CW00362511

Step-by-Step Garden Guides Cottage Gardening

Robert Sulzberger

German-language edition and photographs
Gärtnern leicht und richtig
Bauerngärten
© 1993 BLV Verlagsgesellschaft mbH, München

English-language edition
© 1994 Transedition Books,
a division of Andromeda Oxford
Limited, 11–15 The Vineyard,
Abingdon, Oxfordshire
OX14 3PX

Translation:
Phil Goddard in association with First
Edition Translations Limited, Cambridge
Editing:
Asgard Publishing Services, Leeds
Typesetting:
Organ Graphic, Abingdon

This edition published in the UK in 1994 by Grange Books, an imprint of **Grange Books plc**, The Grange, Grange Yard, London SE1 3AG

Printed in 1994 in Spain

ISBN 1 85627 538 8

Photographic credits
All photographs by the author, except:
J. Harpur 34, 35, 48; Jensen, Glücksburg 64 top left, 64 top right, 65; Kopp/Sulzberger 67, 70, 74 bottom, 90/91; C. Nichols 20; Photos Horticutural frontcover; Redeleit 8, 23 right, 28, 66/67; Reinhard 11 bottom, 13 top, 19, 21, 29 bottom, 30, 33 top, 36, 41, 52, 83; Reinhard-Tierfoto backcover right; H. Smith 2/3, 6/7, 12/13, 24, 26, 50/51, 55, 59, 62/63; The Garden Picture Library (Brigitte Thomas) backcover left

CONTENTS

4 **Introduction**
Life is so much better
nowadays ... or is it?   4

6 **What is a cottage garden?**
The origins and
history of the
cottage garden   6
Cottage gardens
today   10

12 **Minimum maintenance**
Getting the most
out of a small space   12
Nature's fertilisers   14
Natural ways of
providing plant
protection   16

18 **Designing a cottage garden**
Size, shape and
position   18
The right type of
fence   20
Simple, imaginative
home-made fences   22
A welcoming
ceremonial arch   24
Using paths in a
cottage garden   26
Laying down
paved paths   30
The importance
of edging   32
A place for
contemplation   34

36 **Trees, shrubs and fruit**
Trees   36
Life in and around
the orchard   40

The countless
species and
varieties of fruit   42
Creating a structure
with shrubs   44

48 **Climbing and container plants**
Using climbing
plants to cover walls   48
Cottage-style
container plants   50

52 **A riot of colour**
Flowering plants —
attractive and useful   52
Lasting colour in
the cottage garden   54
Annuals and
biennials   60
The rose — queen
of all the flowers   62
The old-fashioned
charm of roses   64

66 **Vegetables, herbs and fruit**
Healthy food from
fertile soil   66
Companion planting
— an old cottage-
garden tradition   68
A selection of
common vegetables   70
Rediscovering lesser-
known vegetables   76
Herbs: a garden full
of year-round flavour   82
Lesser-known herbs   86
Easy-to-grow soft
fruit   90
A cornucopia of
soft fruit   92
Compost — the life-
blood of the garden   94

96 **Index**

Life is so much better nowadays ... or is it?

Times are certainly changing. Not so long ago, many rural homes cultivated a veneer of urban sophistication; in fact some still do. They were painted white, with plain, modern windows. Small, cosy rooms were knocked together into larger ones. Old-fashioned, timeworn wooden furniture was out, and gleaming chrome and leather were in.

Much the same applied to gardens. Immaculately empty patios, neatly trimmed lawns, and a scattering of small shrubs, heathers and dwarf conifers, with perhaps a low-mainten-ance flowerbed full of striking, brightly coloured bedding plants. Perish the thought that old-fashioned plants should be allowed to grow apparently at random.

And vegetables? Why bother with the back-breaking labour suffered by our grandparents, when the supermarkets were full of tinned and frozen food? And of course life was much simpler now we had chemical fertilisers and pesticides. Chemicals gave you big, attractive fruit and vegetables without any of that distasteful manuring. One quick spray got rid of pests, and even traditional weeding was a thing of the past when you could just squirt them with weedkiller.

... or maybe it was better in the good old days

But after decades of believing that technology was the answer to all our problems, things have started to change in the last few years. Overuse of pesticides has started to damage the environ-ment, and people have begun to realise that perhaps their fore-bears had it right after all. Most importantly, people are redis-covering natural ways of con-trolling what goes on in their garden, understanding the relationships between plant growth and the seasons, using the knowledge accumulated by generations of country-dwellers from the observation of nature, and using home-made remedies for garden problems. They may not always be 100 per cent effective, but at least they don't harm the environment.

At the same time, tastes have changed too. The pendulum has swung the other way, and now people immured in the concrete jungle are craving the more romantic approach of the cottage garden. As our living and working environment becomes increasingly treeless and artificial, so people are harking back to the cheerful abundance they remember from their childhood. In an increas-

ingly uncertain and regimented world, the ordered chaos of the cottage garden is a haven of tranquillity. And as we become increasingly aware of the damage we have done to our environment, so the idea of growing your own apples or lettuces has more of an appeal.

The results may not look nearly so big and attractive as their supermarket-bought counterparts, but at least they will have grown to the size they are without the aid of toxic (and therefore potentially dangerous) chemicals.

A reflection of our needs

As our cities become more crowded, the emphasis is moving away from owning large homes. It is becoming increasingly important to have a small part of the great outdoors which we can call our own; somewhere we can retreat to for some fresh air and sunshine. And as this has happened, the cottage garden has become a symbol of the trend away from soulless, ostentatious modernity towards the beauty and simplicity of years gone by. We are starting to become more aware of the healing powers of plants, and more aware of the wider realities that simply don't get taught at school.

So the cottage garden is an expression of inner needs which cannot be met by the material world. But it does not have to be something negative, a refuge from the shortcomings of the outside world. On the contrary, the cottage garden can be something positive which helps us to understand ourselves. It does not have to become a religion, but some of the values which we learn in the garden can benefit us a great deal in our everyday lives outside it.

The cottage garden takes us back to the cheerful simplicity and abundance of bygone days.

The origins and history of the cottage garden

As most historians in the past have shown little interest in humble country-dwellers, much of what we know about the history of the garden comes from important people and events.

The origins of the cottage garden in Europe most likely go back at least two thousand years, beyond the earliest written records. The word 'garden' probably originated among the ancient Germanic peoples of northern Europe, for whom it signified a 'girded' or enclosed place.

Even this far back in time, there appears to have been a clear division between growing fruit and growing vegetables. Fruit was already protected because it grew on trees and so could be left out in the open. But vegetables needed to be fenced in to protect them from the ravages of nature and the predations of hungry geese and chickens, and to keep them separate from wild plants. As time went by, this protected area acquired an important role. It became an extension of the privacy and intimacy of the house, and was protected by law against unwanted visitors.

Increasing the variety of plants

However, much of the credit for the development of the northern European garden is due not to the Germanic peoples but to conquerors from the south. The Romans brought their own highly developed culture with them across the Alps, and this included agriculture.

The choice of vegetables grown in northern Europe was extremely limited. But the Romans brought with them many types of Mediterranean plant to give variety to their meal tables. They also imported many new cultivation techniques, such as the grafting of fruit trees. The word 'propagate' itself comes from the Latin *propagare*.

But people tended to revert to their old habits after the Romans left, and many of the techniques and plants which the Romans brought with them disappeared into the mists of history.

Another major impulse for change came with the capitularies or ordinances issued by Charlemagne — a Frankish king who became emperor over most of continental Western Europe in 800 AD. In his famous *capitulare de villis* he recom-

The plants in a garden often tell us as much about the owner as the walls and the buildings that surround it.

mended which types of plant should be grown. The list included many plants from southern Europe such as cucumbers, melons, rosemary, cumin, fennel and globe artichokes. Charlemagne's decree led his people to grow a much wider variety of plants, and left them healthier and better nourished. Many of these plants are still commonly grown in gardens today (see page 9).

The considerable support which Charlemagne received from the Church did not simply extend to political intrigues. Large numbers of monks migrated to spread Christianity throughout Europe, crossing the Alps and taking more seeds and plants with them.

The monastery garden

The inhabitants of monasteries had to feed themselves, and gardening provided a welcome change from their spiritual rigours. So they developed new and improved techniques of cultivation, including intensive propagation.

Contact between different monasteries meant that newly acquired gardening knowledge could be spread. Monks were also involved in the healing of the sick, and made a number of important discoveries about the healing properties of plants. One influential figure during this period was Hildegard (1098–1179), Abbess of Rupertsberg near the German Rhineland town of Bingen.

Because the monks often had to squeeze much of the garden inside the walls of the monastery, they were the first people to produce sophisticated garden designs. It was the monks who created the strict geometrical designs still typical of many cottage gardens today. The paths were often constructed in the shape of a cross, no doubt to emphasise the meditative aspects of the monks' work. The cross motif was often

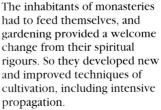

supplemented by a beautiful rose bush at the centre of a circular bed, surrounded by a low evergreen box hedge, symbolising Christ overcoming death on the cross.

These neat geometrical paths are a reminder of the strictly formal design of the monastery garden.

The discovery of beauty

Historical events, both large and small, led to further changes in the garden landscape. The Crusaders brought home flowers and spices from the Middle East along with the trophies of war. As trading routes developed, so knowledge was shared over greater and greater distances. The invention of printing provided a further impetus to the propagation of knowledge, and when Christopher Columbus went to America he opened up a whole new world of hitherto unknown plants. Some of these, such as potatoes, tomatoes, sunflowers and nasturtiums,

have become an essential part of our gardens today.

Box was one of the first common plants to be planted in gardens solely for its decorative and design value. Originally gardens had been mainly a source of food, but over the years affluent people with time on their hands became increasingly interested in the ëpleasure garden' as a place for strolling and personal development. They discovered the beauty of many plants which had no practical use, and realised that species like box were easy to grow and could be cut to shape with a pair of shears. The famous baroque chateau of

the utilitarian kitchen garden to the beauty of the flower garden. Garden styles have also been very much affected by local variations in climates, landscapes and ways of life, and a detailed exploration of all these styles is obviously beyond the scope of a small book like this one. But all good gardeners should use their knowledge of local conditions as a positive source of inspiration.

Versailles near Paris, built by the Sun King, Louis XIV, marked the apex of this new and somewhat artificial form of garden.

As was so often the case, a trend started by the aristocracy gradually filtered down to the ordinary people. Cottage gardens were still largely used to grow plants which could be used in some way; this is the case even today. But people were beginning to allow flowers to creep into their gardens simply on the grounds that they were attractive.

Later still, people turned away from the baroque garden and back towards the relative simplicity and naturalness of the English garden. But looking back through history, the cottage garden incorporates a very wide range of gardening genres, from the strictly formal baroque or monastery garden, through

The cottage-garden tradition dates back to the Middle Ages.

Charlemagne ordered the greatest possible variety of plants to be grown.

The *capitulare de villis* plant list

We require that all manner of plants be grown in gardens, namely:

1. lilium	lily	25. git	nutmeg	48. betas	beet
2. rosas	roses	26. eruca alba	rocket, white	49. vulgigina	hazelwort
3. fenigrecum	fenugreek		mustard	50. mismalvas	marsh mallow
4. costum	spearmint	27. nasturtium	nasturtium	51. malvas	mallow
5. salviam	sage	28. parduna	burdock,	52. carvitas	carrots
6. rutam	rue		plantain	53. pastinacas	parsnips
7. abrotanum	lad's love	29. peludium	pennyroyal	54. adripias	butter leaves
8. cucumeres	cucumbers	30. alisatum	scorzonera	55. blidas	amaranth
9. pepones	melons	31. petresilinum	parsley	56. ravacaulos	kohlrabi
10. cucurbitas	gourds	32. apium	celery	57. caulos	cabbage
11. fasiosum	broad bean	33. leuisticum	lovage	58. uniones	wild garlic
12. ciminum	cumin	34. savinam	savin	59. britlas	chives
13. rosmarinum	rosemary	35. anetum	dill	60. porros	leek
14. careium	caraway	36. fenicolum	fennel	61. radices	radishes
15. cicerum	chick-pea	37. intubas	endives	62. ascalonicas	shallots
16. squillam	sea onion	38. diptamnum	dittany	63. cepas	onions
17. gladiolum	iris	39. sinape	mustard	64. allia	garlic
18. dragantea	arum	40. satureiam	savory	65. warentiam	madder
19. anesum	aniseed	41. sisimbrium	curled mint	66. cardones	cardoon
20. coloquentidas	colocynth,	42. mentam	water mint	67. fabas majores	broad beans
	water melon	43. mentastrum	horsemint	68. pisos Mauriscos	field peas
21. solsequium	water hyacinth	44. tanazitam	tansy	69. coriandrum	coriander
22. ameum	*Ammi majus*	45. neptam	catmint	70. cerfolium	chervil
23. silum	*Laserpitium*	46. febrefugiam	feverfew	71. lacteridas	impatience
24. lactucas	lettuces	47. papaver	poppy	72. sclareian	clary

and the gardener shall also have houseleeks upon his house.

9

Cottage gardens today

Real or imitation?

Different people think of different things when they talk about a cottage garden today. For some, it is neat gravel paths with box hedges surrounding colourful flowerbeds. Others will imagine fences made from gnarled wooden stakes, moss-covered wells and wheelbarrows planted with flowers. Many people associate cottage gardens with elderly women picking fresh vegetables as purring cats and chattering geese look on. And tastes differ.

'A great deal is being written about cottage gardens, and yet I believe that these publications give only a limited insight into the nature of the cottage garden', complains one writer. 'The current image of the cottage garden consists mainly of half-remembered fragments of earlier designs.' That view was expressed in 1937, but it is just as valid today.

So if we are to avoid misunderstandings when talking about cottage gardens, we need to make a very clear distinction between 'real' ones, in a rural setting, and 'imitation' versions in a more urban location.

The 'real' cottage garden is the product of a long tradition. Its carefully designed path layout fits in with the surrounding environment better than it would in a terraced town house. Because there is generally more room available in the country, 'real' cottage gardens are traditionally fenced off into different areas: perhaps a flower garden, a fruit garden and a vegetable garden. In the town version, the relative lack of space means that flowers, fruit and vegetables have to be contained within a single area.

Tomatoes did not appear widely in cottage gardens until this century, and in previous centuries the choice of fruit and vegetables was relatively limited. If you are a cottage gardener, you will often have to ignore many of the changing fashions of town gardens. But it is also wrong to follow the dictates of tradition slavishly and never to move with the times. There's no need for your garden to be turned into a living museum.

The cottage garden: artificial paradise or historical tradition?

Creating a balance between nature and culture

There has been a great deal of controversy over the claim by some environmentalists that you should use only native plants in your gardens, and this applies equally to cottage gardens. Of course it could be argued that country dwellers themselves were the first to grow all these different non-native plants because they were aware of their value as medicines, fertilisers and for other purposes. On the other hand, though, a cottage garden has deliberately been fenced off from the rest of nature for people to enjoy. We do this partly so that we can grow our own food, but also to grow plants solely for their decorative value.

In any case, there have been so many foreign influences on the history of our gardens that it is very difficult to make any meaningful distinction between native and non-native plants. Madonna lilies, Crown Imperial

The bleeding heart: a much-loved import from China.

fritillaries and tulips came from the Middle East. Peonies and bleeding hearts were brought here from China, while plants such as dahlias, sunflowers and American sneezewort crossed the ocean from the New World. But all of them have an established part in our gardens, and our lives, today.

I believe that the most important reason for the appeal of the cottage garden is that it plays such an important part in our childhood memories. The pain of scratching yourself picking blackberries and gooseberries; the pleasure of simple, colourful plants in jungle-like abundance, and the symbolism of plants like the bleeding heart — these are the impressions that stay with us from our childhood and form the basis of the romantic streak which most of us retain. So I believe that the best criteria for including plants in a cottage garden are their childhood associations.

These plants come from all over the world, and yet they still form a harmonious whole.

Getting the most out of a small space

In the past, tending one's garden was often a full-time occupation, and in many cases a question of survival. Today, it has become more of a pleasure than a necessity for most people, and the layout and appearance of cottage gardens has changed accordingly. For many people nowadays, the aim is to produce the most food and flowers in the least space and with the minimum of effort. The size of gardens today is largely dependent on the size of our bank balances and the amount of space available.

There is much that cottage gardens can teach us about the most effective way of achieving these aims. In some cottage gardens, vegetables, flowers and herbs grow apparently higgledy-piggledy. There are two things you need to achieve this appearance of ordered chaos. One is **patience**: the ability to sit back and let the plants grow without interference, and the other is an **awareness** of which plants go well together. For most of us, this awareness does not come naturally and we need to learn it over time from observation and experience.

Some herbs, for example, have a growth habit and root structure which benefit neighbouring vegetables. Growing flowers side-by-side with crops can help the roots to permeate the soil and prevent it from drying out. Flowers can attract beneficial insects and deter pests, and some of them spread so quickly that they smother weeds and reduce the amount of digging and hoeing that needs to be done. And ornamental shrubs can provide a useful combination of colour, shape and ground cover: the art lies in planting them so that they set each other off visually as they come into flower.

There is also a great deal to be gained by recognising wild plants that self-seed in the garden. Some of them can be

Not only do vegetables, herbs and flowers look good when grown together, they can also be beneficial to one another.

The cottage garden was traditionally the province of women.

A shared task

Traditionally, cottage gardens were regarded as the preserve of women. While the man toiled away in the fields, his wife looked after the home, which included the garden.

The reasons used to justify this somewhat dubious division of roles in the past have been many and varied. A woman's place was in the home; women were better at talking to plants to make them grow. Men, on the other hand, had no feeling for attractive combinations of plants, and their overdeveloped sense of order meant they would grow nothing that hadn't been planned beforehand. Also — or so the theory went — women had a greater awareness of the medicinal power of plants and the effects of the passing seasons.

Fortunately times have changed, and so have attitudes to gardening. Tending the plants is a job which is shared between the sexes, and we have realised that men and women have similar needs: a retreat from the daily grind, whether sitting at a desk or looking after children at home; getting your hands dirty and getting some exercise. All of us, men and women alike, benefit from having a little patch of soil to call our own and a place to sit and reflect on the glories of nature.

delicate and attractive if you have an eye for that kind of thing; others have practical advantages, such as orache, which is edible, and greater celandine, whose milky sap is said to cure warts. If you can identify these plants and make use of them, you could end up saving yourself a great deal of unnecessary weeding.

Turning these principles into practice is a long and laborious process which cannot be learned overnight. But one of the main aims of this book is to show you the importance of combining specific plants in a cottage garden.

Nature's fertilisers

Individual requirements

In the past, the only ingredients added to fruit and vegetables were natural ones. Provided it was regularly fed with nutrient-rich farmyard manure, the soil would maintain its long-term fertility.

Unfortunately, animal manure has become a great deal harder to get hold of these days. Even if you live in the country, modern farming techniques and increasing specialisation may mean that this valuable material is no longer available.

If you are fortunate enough to be able to obtain manure, there are some things you should bear in mind. One is not to dig in fresh manure, as it releases toxins into the soil as it rots. Well-rotted manure is much better for the soil than fresh. Also, manure from different animals needs to be treated differently.

Gardening follows exactly the same principles of crop rotation and manuring as agriculture. Different vegetables need different quantities of the rich nutrients that manure contains, and some can actually be harmed by it. Some crops need plenty of fresh manure, while nitrogen-producers like beans and peas

Cabbage and kale in a vegetable plot.

will not tolerate it. Pests can be a problem too: carrots, leeks and onions are often attacked by harmful insects that live in manure.

As crops have different manure requirements, they can be divided into three groups. The first group needs plenty of manure and should be planted immediately after manuring; the second group should be planted about a year later; the third group shouldn't be planted in any location which has been manured in the last two years.

If you aren't able to obtain animal manure, use garden compost instead. This is similar to animal manure as regards its application, except that garden

Group 1: lamb's lettuce (corn salad), radish, beans, peas, herbs

Group 2: lettuce, endive, kohlrabi, swede, kale, beetroot, spinach, Swiss chard, fennel, sweet pepper, aubergine, parsnip, salsify, strawberry, parsley, carrot, onion, leek, garlic

Group 3: cabbage, Brussels sprouts, cauliflower, broccoli, celery, tomato, cucumber, courgette, pumpkin, sweetcorn, potato, rhubarb

NB Individual varieties vary in their requirements, so always consult the seed packet.

compost should be spread annually. So instead of categorising crops as to how long you should wait after application, the categories are based on whether you should use fresh or rotted compost. The first group of vegetables will tolerate compost that has not yet fully rotted; the second group should only be given compost that has been allowed to rot for about a year; and the third group should have no compost directly applied to them at all.

It also does no harm to add some animal manure to your compost, provided you leave it in the compost heap for long enough. All organic materials need time to break down into a rich, dark, uniform mixture before you spread them in the garden.

Regular applications of garden compost are essential for healthy plants.

As you are unlikely to produce enough compost to feed the whole of your garden, you can also buy commercial fertilisers — in which case you should buy organic ones for preference. Dried chicken manure also makes a good substitute for horse manure.

But the best solution of all is to make your own natural liquid fertilisers. These can be made from plants such as nettles and comfrey, and are particularly effective because the nutrients are released into the soil quickly. Liquid feeds are easy to make, although they do smell somewhat unpleasant. All sorts of plants — and especially herbs — can be used to make liquid fertiliser.

Different ways of making your own liquid fertiliser

1   Soak plants in water for 2-4 weeks; fermentation will create foam and an unpleasant smell.

2   Soak plants in water for 24 hours, then simmer on a low heat for 20-30 minutes.

3   Soak plants in cold water for 24 hours, then squeeze out water and strain it before it ferments.

Natural ways of providing plant protection

Obviously there is no real way of proving it, but many natural methods of protecting against pests and weeds are likely to have been tried out first in cottage gardens. There are still people in rural areas who are a mine of useful information about ways of protecting fruit, vegetables and flowers against these threats without upsetting the balance of nature. And most experienced gardeners have their own homespun recipes for getting rid of things like mice, slugs, snails and mildew. Generations of experience have shown that no one does the job of keeping plants healthy more effectively than Mother Nature.

The three most important ways of doing this are proper feeding (see previous page), crop rotation, and effective watering. Different types of plants can be combined to provide ground cover and to keep down weeds, and some plants will deter pests from attacking their neighbours.

Plants which protect other plants

Some experienced cottage gardeners will deliberately allow some of their vegetables to go to seed. Apart from providing seed for next year's crop, the flowers can also attract beneficial insects. They may also grow certain flowers specifically to attract pests, so that they can then pick them off by hand. For example butterflies, including the familiar cabbage white, are particularly fond of dahlias, hyssop and candytuft.

Euphorbia lathyris is another plant not often seen except in cottage gardens, where it has the advantage of repelling voles. Garlic and Crown Imperial fritillaries both smell unpleasant and are reputed to have this ability too, though they are not 100 per cent effective.

A simple and effective 'scarecrow' made from potatoes and feathers.

If you place broom twigs between rows of radishes and cabbage seedlings they will deter flea beetles, while mustard planted between rows of vegetables is believed to keep slugs and snails away. These voracious pests also tend to congregate on planks used as edging for paths, where they can easily be picked off: another fact which must have been discovered in the cottage garden. And another well-known rural remedy is the beer trap with a lid. This means that the beer is not watered down when it rains, which is precisely when slugs and snails come out.

Farmers and cottage gardeners also have their own ways of scaring off hungry birds. In the open fields, a scarecrow may be the answer: it will prove very popular with children even if birds sometimes seem to ignore it completely. In the garden, you could try hanging up a cat mask. One other very simple and effective way of scaring off birds is to hang five or six potatoes on a stout stick, and then push feathers into the potatoes so that the structure moves in the slightest breeze.

Poultry have some less obvious uses. If you let ducks, geese or chickens roam in your garden, you're unlikely to have a problem with slugs.

Many simple home-made liquid fertilisers and sprays can be made using old country recipes. Farmers used to mix clay, chalk, cow manure and plants such as tansy and horsetail to make an effective pesticide which was then painted onto the stems of plants. Diluted whey makes a good fungicide spray for tomatoes and other plants, and many herbs contain substances which repel insects.

Left *A slug trap with a lid — an old country idea.*

Below *Ducks are one of the best ways of dealing with a slug problem.*

Size, shape and position

In a traditional village you are likely to find a stream, hedgerows, a village pond, plenty of large trees and an orchard. In addition, each house will have its own cultivation plot, and may also have an enclosed front garden. So people have all the main things they need within easy reach, and the area has a balanced ecology.

The trouble is that there are not as many traditional villages as there used to be. Settlement patterns and lifestyles have changed; farming has become more intensive, an many hedge-rows have vanished. But the true cottage garden, as opposed to the imitation version created in a more urban setting, still has a symbiotic, interdependent relationship with its surroundings. One of the most essential features of a real cottage garden is that it doesn't need to contain any of the features listed above because they are located nearby. The landscape may well have been affected by the ravages of the 20th century, but it is still likely to contain trees, hedgerows, water and similar features.

An imitation cottage garden doesn't have these advantages. The nearest fruit may be in the local supermarket; the nearest trees in a park a mile away. Birds, insects and other useful creatures may have to be lured into the garden by planting specific shrubs and flowers.

A real cottage garden is also unlikely to contain a pond or stream, unless it is a natural one, perhaps coming from a spring. An artificial pond can radically change the character of a garden, and so doesn't really

A true cottage garden contains flowers and vegetables, but not trees, as there are plenty of these in the immediate vicinity.

belong in a true cottage garden — though of course if you want your own pond, then by all means have one: your personal tastes are more important than the dictates of fashion.

Small is beautiful

Most of us don't have much choice as to the size of our gardens. By the time you've fitted in a tree, a hedge and a few fruit bushes, there may not be much space left.

In fact, though, it's surprising just how small a successful cottage garden can be. The smallest space in which it is realistically possible to create one is about 30 sq yd (25 m²). If you are lucky enough to have a garden measuring 300 sq yd (250 m²) or more, you can still make a reasonably authentic-looking cottage garden, perhaps with shrubs and trees, and wide, box hedge-lined paths. But you lose some of the intimacy of the real cottage garden. The ideal size is around 120 sq yd (100 m²).

As a rule, a cottage garden should be square or rectangular, even if you adopt the traditional design consisting of two paths crossing in the centre and circular or oval paths round the edge (see page 27). Ideally, an authentic cottage garden shouldn't come right up to the house itself. Instead, there should be a transition from house to garden, maybe containing a bench, cordon fruit trees or climbing plants, a flower bed and some container plants. In an imitation cottage

Tall shrubs and perennials growing against the fence to create height.

garden you may not have enough space, so these items will need to be integrated within the garden as a whole.

A south-facing garden

Ideally your vegetable and herb garden should be facing south, or at a pinch south-east or south-west. Many crops, such as tomatoes, cucumbers, fennel and herbs, come from warm countries and need as much sun and warmth as possible. If you have a shady garden, there are plenty of attractive plants you can put in it, but it is more difficult to reproduce the typical features of a cottage garden. A sheltered suntrap, where the soil warms up quickly in spring, will afford more varied and numerous plants.

Another very important requirement for a cottage garden is that it should include not just flower beds and paths, but also tall-growing plants, to create a three-dimensional effect.

 One relatively easy way of creating height is to use specimen shrubs. Some of the species suitable for a cottage garden are listed from page 44 onwards.

Biennials — e.g. hollyhocks, foxgloves and verbascum — can also be used to fill in the gaps in the design. And a fence not only helps to keep out unwanted visitors; it also provides an essential framework for the garden.

The right type of fence

As we have seen, the wall or fence is an important part of all gardens, and particularly of the cottage garden. The fence is one of the first things visitors notice, and so it is worth giving some thought to the kind of fence which will best suit your garden.

Whatever material you use, the fence should be lower than is normally the case in most gardens. In an authentic cottage garden the fence should encourage the viewer to look across and beyond it to the surrounding countryside; it should not be an obstacle. Its protective function today is more symbolic than real. If you need to keep chickens, ducks or rabbits out of the garden, the fence need only be somewhere around 2 ft (50–80 cm) high. The only case where you will need a fence much over 3 ft (1 m) high is if you have deer problems.

One material commonly used in the country is chicken wire. This is even sometimes used in authentic cottage gardens, probably for the simple reason that it is cheap and easy to transport. Just add a few concrete or steel posts, and you have your fence.

As you are trying to recreate the simple, utilitarian effect of a cottage garden, there is nothing wrong with using chicken wire. It can sometimes look quite attractive as it weathers, with climbing roses sprawled over it and other flowers peeking through the holes. However, if yours is a suburban cottage garden, then more natural materials are better.

Natural wood
The obvious choice is wood. Whether you use closeboard, post and rail, picket or ranch-style fencing, wood is a natural material which blends in with the landscape and can often enhance the rustic feel of a cottage garden. You may well have to combine wood with other, man-made, materials such as concrete posts — although it is possible to buy concrete fence posts that are also attractive (see page 23). But the main rule to follow is use whichever materials are easiest to obtain in your particular area. If you live in northern Britain, for example, you may be able to obtain enough suitable stones to build a low dry-stone wall, which need only be about 2 ft 8 in (80 cm) high. This can look particularly attractive with plants growing above. Alternatively, you might build a low stone wall with a wooden fence on top for added height.

A cottage garden needs no more than a simple wooden fence.

20

aren't cheap — keep to traditional designs, and don't be tempted to follow short-term vagaries of fashion. Modern designs may look good now, but they may look dated in ten years' time, and they don't fit the cottage-garden style.

Use local materials

Where possible, try to use local materials. Stone walls may not be compatible with the traditional cottage-garden style, but they may still be most appropriate if they are traditional in the area where you live. The same applies to hedges. In more exposed coastal regions, for example, a thick hedge around the garden may be essential to provide the necessary shelter for your plants.

One very attractive fencing material is wrought ironwork. Where a garden has an old wrought-iron fence, this often shows that previous owners valued it highly. A carefully tended wrought-iron fence can look very elegant, and even a neglected one may look highly authentic, having the attractive patina that comes with age.

If you do decide to invest in a wrought-iron fence — and they

A wrought-iron fence shows that the owner believes the garden is worth spending money on.

Two examples of traditional wrought-iron designs.

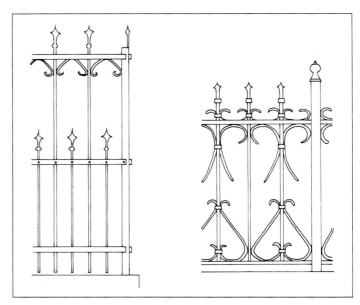

Simple, imaginative home-made fences

The oldest known garden fences were woven from thin branches, mostly of willow. There were two main forms: horizontal, with wooden posts about 3 ft (1 m) apart and branches woven between them, and vertical, which used long cross-pieces. This type of fence is rarely seen today because the techniques used to make them have been largely forgotten. If you do manage to make one of these fences, you can pride yourself in not having used any nails, screws, or other modern aids in its construction.

Alternatively, you could build yourself a fence made of simple vertical posts or boards; semi-circular poles tapered at the top look more attractive than plain ones. Use two cross-pieces, with the distance between them being about half the height of the fence. Nail the stakes to them at intervals of about 1.5 in (3-4 cm).

Originality is the key
Some garden centres and do-it-yourself stores sell ready-made fences made from diagonally crossed stakes. But many purists dislike these on the grounds that their rustic appearance is contrived and artificial. They just do not fit in with the simple, natural look of the cottage garden.

You can make a more natural-looking fence using unplaned boards, which have the advantage of being irregularly shaped and showing off the form of the tree trunk. Use these to make

Original and cheap to make yourself: woven fences.

two or three parallel cross-pieces attached at intervals to vertical posts. Or, for an even more home-made look, try round stakes cut lengthwise with the bark still left on the outside. Place the bark side facing out of the garden. Obviously this type of fence will not provide an effective barrier to stop wild animals getting in or poultry getting out, but it is an attractive way of simply marking out the edge of the garden.

Fence posts: sturdy and rotproof
If the uprights are made of wood, they should be buried at least 1 ft 4 in (40 cm) deep. If you use a heavy fence, it will probably need concrete foundations. Also, the wooden parts which are in direct contact with

Even in the simplest of fences, wood imparts a natural charm.

If you have to use concrete posts, it is possible to obtain attractive ones.

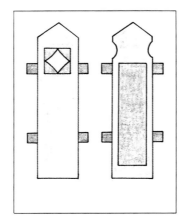

the ground will need long-term rotproofing. Those which are not touching the ground need not be coated. Use a non-toxic preservative rather than the usual creosote, which can be fatal to plants and animals.

In addition to, or perhaps instead of, applying a preservative, you might like to try an old country trick: singe the buried end of the board or pole with a flame. This creates a layer of soot, which makes a very effective protection against rotting.

23

A welcoming ceremonial arch

A flower-covered arch over the entrance to the garden provides an impressive welcome for visitors, and gives them, and perhaps even you, a foretaste of the pleasures in store beyond.

The simplest arches are made from wood, and need not necessarily be semicircular. A rectangular wooden framework can look just as good when covered in climbing plants, while if you are creating a new cottage garden from scratch, you might consider using an iron or wrought-iron arch. If the arch is a heavy, high-quality one, it is probably a good idea to set it in concrete foundations. Otherwise, place the feet of the arch in a hole about 1 ft 6 in (40–50 cm) deep, wedge them in with stones and tread the soil down firmly after filling in the hole.

A royal welcome — an archway grown with climbing roses.

This glass globe makes an eye-catching foil for plants.

A riot of colour and fragrance

The most popular climbing plants used for this purpose have traditionally been climbing roses, clematis and honeysuckle. These should ideally be planted beside the arch in October or November while the soil is still soft enough — maybe one plant on either side.

Clematis hybrids, with their big bright blue, pink and white flowers, should be planted with their heads in the sun and their feet in the shade; in other words, the base of the plant should be covered by other plants or a mulch to keep the sun off the roots.

Honeysuckle is a good choice because of the strongly scented flowers of some species: *Lonicera periclymenum* 'Belgica', *L. p.* 'Serotina' or the brilliant yellow *L. p.* 'Graham Thomas' are particularly good in this respect. *L. henryi* is less fragrant, but has the advantage of being partially evergreen.

Climbing roses will need to be pruned in early spring, when you can see which shoots, if any, have been damaged by frost. Cut these out, together with one or two of the older stems, down to ground level. Instead of climbing roses, you might place **standard roses** on either side of the entrance: the effect might not be quite so grand, but it still provides a stylish welcome for visitors.

Using coloured glass

A glass ball mounted on a pole and glinting in the sun is bound to draw admiring comments from visitors. Inevitably, the next thing they will want to know is its precise significance, which is not an easy question to answer.

It is known that in 13th-century Italy glass balls were a symbol of fertility and were used to decorate people's homes. Here, their main use is at Christmas, but they also make attractive garden decorations and are sometimes sold in garden centres. Once finely hand-blown, they are now mass-produced in the Far East.

In legend these 'crystal balls', which reflect the surrounding landscape and the sun, are a bringer of good luck and were used to drive away demons and evil spirits. On a more prosaic note, it has been suggested that they may prevent frost damage to plants by storing up heat during the day and releasing it at night. More plausibly, they may act as bird-scarers by reflecting the sunlight.

Using paths in a cottage garden

The main difference between a cottage garden and a 'normal' garden is that the former does not normally include a lawn, fruit trees, or a specific area of shrubs. Also, there is no clear division in a cottage garden between herbaceous borders and the vegetable and herb areas.

In an ordinary garden there may be no path at all, or a winding path may be deliberately used to achieve a natural, random look. Not so the cottage garden: the apparent chaos of vegetables, flowering plants and herbs is held together by a strictly geometrical, and usually symmetrical system of paths. The paths are normally straight, providing a strong visual link between the different parts of the garden and bringing a sense of order, both visually and physically.

One main path with others leading off it

The simplest layout for the standard rectangular or square cottage garden is a main path through the centre with others branching off it at intervals of one bed's width. The main path should be about 2-4 ft (60-120 cm) wide so that you can move around the garden with wheelbarrows and other implements.

Some people with slightly larger gardens use a minor variation on this layout. Here, there is a second rectangular path enclosing the first one, and running parallel with the fence about a flower bed's width away from it. This secondary path should be around 1 ft 6 in (40-50 cm) wide. In this common variation, the inner

A straight path through the roses retains an air of informality.

rectangle contains vegetables and annuals, while the outer beds adjoining the fence are used to grow herbaceous perennials dotted with the occasional shrub. This system has the advantage that the whole of the centre area can be dug over in the autumn.

The standard width for a bed is around 4 ft (1.2 m), which is the distance most people can reach easily. If you have problems reaching the whole of the central area, you might put other, narrower paths in the middle. These should be placed so that you can access everywhere that you need to, and need only be about 1 ft (20–30 cm) wide. Use planks, duckboards or thin concrete paving for these paths.

Crossed paths: the focal point of the cottage garden

The traditional monastery garden centred on the point where the paths between the cloisters crossed. Two main paths crossing at right angles in the centre of the garden, with other narrower paths branching off them, are generally regarded as typical of the cottage garden. To make it even more authentic, you might place a circular island bed at its centre, perhaps containing a fountain, statue, sundial or even a tree. However as a

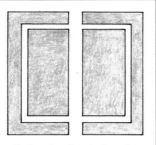

Single main path and outer path

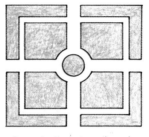

Crossed paths, outer paths and central circular bed

Oval outer path

Diamond-shaped path

tree may cast too much shadow, it should be the exception rather than the rule.

The most common central feature used in this type of garden is a beautiful shrub rose or standard rose, ideally underplanted with lavender or another suitable plant. The arrangement might also include a glass ball to catch the light (see page 25). Madonna lilies make another striking feature for this central position, and monks often used other plants which symbolised the Cross and the Resurrection.

The crossed paths divide the area into four, which also has another practical advantage: the four beds are ideally suited to a crop rotation system. One bed can be used for root crops, one for legumes and salad vegetables, one for brassicas and one for more permanent crops.

Obviously there are plenty of other ways in which you can arrange your paths: depending on the shape of your garden, you might lay them out in a diamond shape within the outer fence, or even have round or oval outer paths. The choice is yours: the only important requirement is that the layout should be strictly geometrical.

The centre of the garden provides a focus for neat, clearly edged paths.

which allow air and water to permeate through them create a natural and attractive micro-climate. Hard paths have no place in the traditional cottage garden — and in any case, soft surfaces invariably look much more attractive in this rural-style environment than a cold stone surface.

The easiest solution is simply to have bare soil. What happens in many cottage gardens is that the paths are dug over along with the whole of the rest of the garden in autumn, and laid out again in spring, with the paths trodden down well. This system means that weeds can easily be raked out, and if necessary you can cover the paths with planks or boards. These are now available in recycled plastic which, unlike wood, is completely weatherproof.

Don't use hard paths

Another important feature of the cottage garden is that the paths should ideally be soft, not hard. Even if you are a city-dweller, there are other ways of protecting your feet in wet weather than paving stones, concrete or asphalt. Surfaces

Neat gravel

A path covered with fine gravel looks both natural and neat, and goes particularly well with box parterres or low hedges. The gravel should be at least 1-2 in (3-5 cm) deep, and should be regularly raked over to cover bare patches and smooth out bumps. The weeds will still grow up through the gravel, but they can be pulled out relatively easily.

Alternatively, you might use slightly larger pebbles, though they should not be so large and round that walking on them is uncomfortable. Or if you have access to reasonably cheap coarse sand, by all means use it. This will need to be tidied and raked from time to time, but, as in the case of gravel, weeding it is normally a fairly easy process.

A gravel path looks neat, while bark mulch creates a woodland atmosphere with its scent.

The pleasant scent of bark chippings

Bark mulches have become very popular in recent years for creating the natural garden look. They are particularly attractive in cottage gardens, and are made from shredded, but not rotted, bark. This blends in with the surroundings and gives off a very pleasant woody smell. It also makes it harder for weeds to take over. A bark mulch is best laid with a layer of gravel underneath; like all soft surfaces, it will need some kind of retaining edge to stop it from drifting into the flower beds.

Bark mulch has appeared on the garden scene only relatively recently. Its predecessor was tanbark, a waste product of tanneries which had the same useful properties as bark mulch when shredded.

Laying down paved paths

If you do use hard, paved paths, make sure you use a natural-looking material. You should normally place a 4–8-in (10–20-cm) layer of hardcore underneath to give the path stability and allow water to drain away. The same applies to other surfaces such as bark chippings, sand or fine gravel.

The most suitable type of hard surfacing for any large, grand garden is granite setts or natural stone flags. Most specialist suppliers will sell these in a variety of colours, but you should give preference to whichever forms of natural stone are commonly used as a building material in your area. These will also often be the cheapest.

Stone flags should be laid in a layer of sand, fitted as close together as possible for stability. Fill any gaps with sand.

One cheaper way of paving a path is to use bricks, which may after all be lying around unused, left over from building something else. Bricks have a rich, warm look to them, and will provide a perfect match with a brick house.

Lay the bricks on sand, either face down or on their edges. They may weather and crack with time, and moss and other plants may grow between them, but this look can be quite appropriate in a cottage garden. One problem, however, is that deep-rooted weeds such as dandelions may be impossible to get rid of completely.

A paved path should normally be built on solid foundations.

Above *A water container is an essential feature of the cottage garden.*

Right *Different ways of constructing a path.*

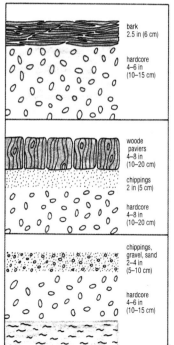

bark
2.5 in (6 cm)

hardcore
4–6 in
(10–15 cm)

woode
paviers
4–8 in
(10–20 cm)

chippings
2 in (5 cm)

hardcore
4–8 in
(10–20 cm)

chippings,
gravel, sand
2–4 in
(5–10 cm)

hardcore
4–6 in
(10–15 cm)

One relatively new product on the market is sealed wooden paviers, often sold in round, square or rectangular shapes. They are obviously not part of the traditional cottage garden; but because they are a completely natural material, they can look very good in one, and are definitely worth considering. One thing to bear in mind, however, is that they become fairly slippery when wet.

Access to water

While a hose can provide a jarring note of modernity in a supposedly traditional garden, a water container, perhaps with a nice metal watering-can beside it, is one of the typical features of a cottage garden. It helps to save water and also helps to humidify the air around it. From an ecological point of view, the best place to put the container is beside the house so that rainwater drains into it. However, it will often be more convenient to place the container at the centre of the garden so that you do not have to carry the watering can too far in any direction; water in the centre of the garden may also be said to symbolise the source of life. Alternatively you could put the container in an attractive corner of the cottage garden.

The water container might be a walled trough, a plastic or (preferably) a wooden barrel, or even concrete rings from a building site. Connect the container to a tap via an underground pipe, placed at least 1 ft (about 30–40 cm) deep in the soil where frost will not affect it. You will then be able to get a suitable mixture of tap water and rainwater which can be used for watering the garden.

The importance of edging

Flower and vegetable beds need some kind of edging to bring a sense of ordered calm to the apparent chaos of the cottage garden. The simplest form of edging is some kind of brick, board or other material which ensures that soil is not washed onto the paths and that gravel does not get kicked into the flower beds. Edging also prevents plants from spreading onto the paths, and weeds from colonising the vegetable plot.

Natural stone can look very good, whether in the form of square or rectangular quarry stone, or as irregular rock pieces. If the subsoil is not very stable, you may need to plant the larger stones in a layer of sand or even concrete.

Concrete, often available in the form of elaborate **paving setts**, is itself a practical edging material, and does not look too out of place, especially when overgrown with plants. But it does not totally fit in with the style of a cottage garden. Nor does corrugated plastic lawn

edging, even if it is green, though price is one point in its favour. The **wire mesh** edging often sold in garden centres is not particularly suitable either.

Wooden edging goes particularly well with bark-mulch paths. One cheap and simple form of edging is boards placed

on their edges in the soil. If pressure-treated with fungicide they will last for many years. Railway sleepers or logs will last even longer, and can be treated to last almost indefinitely.

Evergreen box parterres are one of the most typical features of the cottage garden.

A path edged with flowering marigolds.

Box hedging — the ideal edging for cottage gardens

Box doesn't seem to have found favour with Charlemagne — at least, it doesn't feature in his *capitulare de villis* (see page 9) — but it is actually known to have been used in gardens for thousands of years.

Although box is regarded as a typical cottage-garden plant, it doesn't suit every small garden. In narrow beds, the large area of green hedging can upstage the plants themselves. In this case its benefits may be limited, and it may be hard to justify using it.

If you do choose box as an edging plant, use the cultivar 'Suffruticosa', which even if you neglect to prune it in spring will not grow to more than 3 ft (1 m) or so in height. The best time to plant it is March or April, and it can be planted in any soil which is not excessively wet or dry.

Box is also easy to propagate. Take heel cuttings in the autumn (September/October), insert them in a well-drained compost and overwinter them outdoors in a sheltered position.

Obviously, the best form of edging for a cottage garden is the natural kind. **Low-growing flowering plants** such as alpine phlox, alyssum or creeping thyme serve this purpose very well. Another strongly scented plant, lavender, not only looks very good in company with roses, but is also used as an edging plant.

Some **biennials** have also traditionally been used as edging. These include forget-me-nots, pansies and daisies — all of them easy to propagate, and free-flowering from spring to late summer. However, these plants will need to be resown every year (see page 60).

A place for contemplation

Sitting down in the garden, putting your feet up and contemplating the fruits of your labours has always been one of life's great pleasures. Any cottage garden worthy of the name should include somewhere, perhaps a bench, where you can indulge this pleasure. If you put a bench against a south-facing wall, you will be able to use it in the evenings, and in spring and autumn when it might otherwise be too cold to sit out. This is because the wall acts like a storage heater, absorbing heat from the sun during the day and releasing it

into the air when the surroundings are cooler.

Most garden furniture is stable and weather-resistant. If necessary, buy folding or collapsible furniture, but whatever you do, buy wooden, not plastic. This is one of the most important requirements for a cottage garden. A bench made from parallel horizontal boards has a simple, harmonious effect. Benches made from halved logs create a rather more hand-hewn, rustic effect but will only fit into certain types of garden. Add a table, and this will not only look better, but will also encourage

Arbours needn't be just a place for sitting in. One other possible use is as a shelter for a barbecue, which is entirely feasible provided it fits in with the rest of the garden. Use plain brick or even natural stone to make the barbecue stand.

A place to sit and admire the beauty of a garden in bloom.

This arbour provides a quiet retreat amid the greenery.

you to use the garden as a place for eating or even working and playing. Obviously you should make sure that the table, and any other furniture, matches the bench.

The surfacing you use for this area will also have to fit in with its surroundings. Gravel is perhaps the most obvious choice, and quarried stone or granite setts are perfectly acceptable as well. What you shouldn't have are those large expanses of the grey concrete paving stones that are commonly associated with modern estates.

Building an arbour

A cottage garden needs somewhere to sit down, and an arbour in the middle of the garden may be ideal, especially if you do not have a south-facing wall to place a bench against. As well as looking good from outside, an arbour provides shade and seclusion with its carpet of foliage and flowers, and gives you an all-round view of the garden as a whole.

The best material to use for the basic framework is stripped, painted or treated poles, with an inner framework of narrow boards. Obviously a ready-made wrought-iron structure is more elegant and durable. It even looks smart on its own without any plants growing on it, where-

as a wooden arbour is primarily used to train climbing plants. The flowers will make it look attractive, and the foliage creates privacy.

The best plants to grow round the entrance are climbing roses, clematis or some honeysuckle species, providing a combination of both colour and scent. Virginia creeper and Dutchman's pipe (*Aristolochia*) are particularly suitable for covering arbours because of their profuse

greenery. In warmer and more sheltered areas you might try a grapevine, which might even provide a hint of decadence by dangling bunches of grapes into the mouth of the visitor! Russian vine (*Fallopia baldschuanica*, syn. *Polygonatum baldschuanica*) is another possibility, though it is very fast-growing. But if the emphasis is on a natural-looking cottage garden, you should preferably use native plants instead.

Trees

Unlike houses on many modern estates, traditional cottages are rarely surrounded by treeless wastes. On the contrary, trees and shrubs provide a link with the surrounding countryside.

In some circumstances it is possible to grow a tall tree near to the house, towering over it, and providing symbolic protection for the inhabitants as well as a reminder of the changing seasons. Often this protection is not purely symbolic: in coastal areas especially, trees provide vital shelter from gales.

On the other hand, trees take up a great deal of space and light, and are therefore best kept well away from the garden. On a village green, for example, some large and beautiful trees may provide a unifying link for the whole village, just like the spreading chestnut tree in Henry Longfellow's poem *The Village Blacksmith*.

Inside or outside the garden?
For these reasons, trees have not traditionally formed a part of the cottage garden, and have tended to be kept outside it. Another major reason is that, in our climate, plants need all the warmth and sunlight they can get, and so shaded gardens are not so desirable as they are in some other countries.

In the average imitation cottage garden, the question is unlikely to arise anyway, as the garden will probably be small and a large tree will simply not fit in. In a much larger garden there may be space for a tree-shaded area, which can be used to house the compost heap — and perhaps a collection of shade-loving perennials to provide a country atmosphere.

If you have the space, a large tree can provide very good shelter for the house.

In a smaller garden, you will probably have to make do with a smaller tree such as a fruit tree.

Use small trees ...

There are plenty of smaller trees which can be grown in a more confined space. Examples include various species of *Sorbus* such as the rowan or mountain ash, whitebeam and service tree, whose berries all have a high vitamin-C content. Other examples include hawthorn, pink hawthorn, robinia and the plane tree. Birches are often used in cottage gardens, but their shallow roots tend to spread over a large area, so they are probably not suited to a smaller, closely planted garden.

Most bush fruit trees reach only a moderate height and are suitable for the smaller garden. They include apples, pears, cherries, plums and gages. The medlar is unfortunately rarely found these days, though quinces, with their fragrant fruit, are still to be seen, especially in fruit-growing areas. If you are really short of space,

the alternative to growing a tree is to create a similar effect by growing climbing plants up the side of the house, or with cordon-grown fruit.

The walnut tree is somewhat borderline as far as height is concerned, as it will eventually reach 60 or even 100 ft (20–30 m). But if you have room for one, it is in many ways an ideal large tree. Apart from its attractive appearance, the tree also provides thousands of nuts, and the scent of its leaves is reputed to keep harmful insects at bay.

... or large trees ...

In a large garden or courtyard, you can afford to choose a particularly big tree which will form a centrepiece for the whole house. The various species of lime tree look particularly imposing and have earned themselves a place in poetry and legend, while a giant ash called Yggdrasill was referred to in Norse mythology. The oak is the most characteristic feature of the English countryside, and other large native trees commonly grown in large gardens include the wych and English elm, sycamore and oak. The distinctive growth habit of the weeping willow makes it a good specimen tree, while the chest-

 The leaves of trees such as walnut, oak, chestnut, beech, poplar and birch contain tannins which slow down the decomposition process. Dead leaves also upset the balance of the compost heap simply because there are so many of them. So they should be composted separately using nitrogenous compost accelerators.

nut, originally from the Middle East, has been widely planted in European parks and gardens, and is popular for the cool shade provided by its dense foliage.

... but not conifers!

Whatever you do, don't plant any of the countless species of conifers. Their cool elegance is simply not suited to the warmth and disarray of the cottage garden, although obviously these things are a matter of taste. Deciduous trees may create shade in the house and garden in summer, but at least, unlike evergreen conifers, they have the good grace to shed their leaves in winter so that they don't create unnecessary shade when it's least wanted. The table below does not include conifers.

Garden trees

English name	Botanical name	Height in ft (m)	Site	Remarks
Smaller trees				
hawthorn	*Crataegus laevigata*	6-20 (2-6)	sun/light shade	some varities have double flowers
hawthorn	*Crataegus monogyma*	6-20 (2-6)	sun/light shade	white flowers
field maple	*Acer campestre*	30-50 (10-15)	full sun, any good soil	attracts insects and birds
mountain ash, rowan	*Sorbus aucuparia*	25-40 (8-12)	sun/light shade	bright-red berries
robinia	*Robinia pseudoacacia*	10-30 (3-10)	sun/light shade	can be trimmed to shape
service tree	*Sorbus domestica*	30-50 (10-15)	sun, not too wet	fruit can be stored and eaten
whitebeam	*Sorbus aria*	25-40 (8-12)	sun/slight shade	orange-red berries

English name	Botanical name	Height in ft (m)	Site	Remarks
Fruit trees				
apple	*Malus domestica*	12-20 (4-6)	sun, deep well-drained soil	most need pollination partner
cherry	*Prunus avium*	12-25 (4-8)	deep, free-draining soil	self-fertilising varities best
medlar	*Mespilus germanica*	12-20 (4-6)	sun/light shade	store fruits before eating
pear	*Pyrus communis*	30-50 (10-15)	sunny, sheltered	most need pollination partner
plum	*Prumus × domestica*	16-23 (5-7)	sheltered, free-draining soil	dessert and culinary varieties; also gages
cherry plum (myrobalan)	*Prunus cerasifera*	16-23 (5-7)	sun, humus-rich soil	small, light-yellow fruits
quince	*Cydonia oblonga*	12-20 (4-6)	humus-rich soil	scented fruit
walnut	*Juglans regia*	50-100 (15-30)	sun, deep well-drained soil	nuts appear after about 10 years
Larger trees				
ash	*Fraxinus excelsoir*	130 (40)	sun or partial shade	smaller garden varieties available
wych elm	*Ulmus glabra*	100-130 (30-40)	sun or partial shade	subject to Dutch elm disease
Cornish elm	*Ulmus minor* 'Cornubiensis'	100-130 (30-40)	more tolerant of poor soil	subject to Dutch elm disease
horse chestnut	*Aesculus hippocastanum*	60-100 (20-30)	full sun	creates deep shade
small-leaved lime	*Tilia cordata*	50-100 (15-30)	sun or partial shade	flowers attract bees (but can also be toxic to them)
large-leaved lime	*Tilia platyphyllos*	100-130 (30-40)	sun or partial shade	flowers attract bees (but can also be toxic to them)
Norway maple	*Acer platanoides*	60-130 (20-40)	full sun	very hardy and tolerant
common oak	*Quercus robur*	60-100 (20-30)	full sun, deep soil	'Concordia' reaches only 32 ft (10 m)
sessile oak	*Quercus petraea*	100-130 (30-40)	full sun, deep soil	similar to common oak
plane	*Platanus × acerifolia*	60-100 (20-30)	sun or partial shade	pollution-resistant
sycamore	*Acer pseudoplatanus*	60-100 (20-30)	full sun	very fast-growing
weeping willow	*Salix alba* 'Tristis'	50-60 (15-20)	full sun, damp soil	smaller varieties available

Life in and around the orchard

Until a few decades ago, the only fruit trees grown were full-sized ones. These had to be planted outside people's gardens because they were so large, either along the side of a road or in an orchard. They were only rarely pruned, and the small fruits were mainly picked up as windfalls, so were not suitable for use as table fruit. Some people preferred to use their fruit to make juice, cider or perry, or fruit wine.

The fact that these trees were not intensively cultivated also meant that they received little attention from humans, and were not sprayed. This meant that the orchard became an attractive home for animals and plants that were threatened elsewhere.

Old full-size trees provide both a home and a source of food to insects, birds and some species of mammals. The hollows in the trees are a nesting place for owls, bats, woodpeckers and dormice. And rotting branches may be home to huge numbers of beetles and their larvae. The grass underneath contains many flowering plants whose nectar attracts bees, butterflies and other insects. So if your cottage garden does contain grass, consider letting it grow and perhaps creating a meadow by planting a wild flower mixture, rather than having a neatly tended ornamental lawn.

Most of us have to do without a full-sized orchard.

Older trees may provide homes for endangered animal species such as little owls and small mammals like the dormouse.

Planting fruit trees

Leave plenty of space between fruit trees to allow them to spread: exactly how much will depend on the species. The best time to plant fruit trees is in autumn when they have lost their leaves. Prune the shoots and loose roots back by about a third. Dig over the bottom of the hole to loosen the soil, and surround the roots with plenty of well-rotted garden compost. If necessary, place a stake on the southern side of the trunk before planting the tree; this can then be attached to the tree by a tree tie later on.

In recent years, fruit trees have been bred for ever-decreasing size. This means that nowadays there is one to fit into almost any garden. So if you are planning your own imitation cottage garden, there is no reason why it shouldn't include its own miniature orchard.

Ask the nursery for advice on which rootstock is best suited to your particular garden, telling them the maximum size you want it to grow and the variety of fruit you prefer. Unlike trees in orchards left to their own devices, a dwarf tree will need careful pruning, especially during its first few years. Try growing soil-improving plants such as lupins, phacelia or marigolds; nasturtiums are reputed to keep harmful insects away from trees.

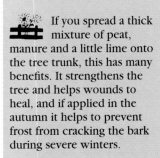 If you spread a thick mixture of peat, manure and a little lime onto the tree trunk, this has many benefits. It strengthens the tree and helps wounds to heal, and if applied in the autumn it helps to prevent frost from cracking the bark during severe winters.

41

The countless species and varieties of fruit

The serviceberry, quince, medlar and damson are all once-popular species of fruit which have become increasingly uncommon today.

The **service tree** (*Sorbus domestica*) prefers a dry, sunny position and alkaline soil. It is closely related to the mountain ash or rowan tree, but has larger fruits. Because they have such a very high tannic-acid content, serviceberries cannot be eaten until they become really soft and squashy. For very similar

reasons, they are sometimes used in wine-making.

The **quince** (*Cydonia oblonga*), like the service tree, may have either apple- or pear-shaped fruits. Quinces are golden-yellow, and their most distinctive feature is their strong scent. Their main use is in making quince jelly as they have a high pectin content.

The highly versatile **medlar** (*Mespilus germanica*) has highly attractive fruit and large white flowers.

Finally, the **damson** (*Prunus institia*) is a thorny tree or bush, derived long ago from a cross between a sloe and a cherry plum. The flesh of the red, yellow or mauve fruits doesn't come away from the stone as easily as that of its cultivated relatives.

Choose a suitable variety for local conditions

There is a bewildering number of varieties of fruit, particularly apples, available today. You can choose varieties which are less susceptible to late frosts, or more resistant to disease; which ripen early or late; which vary in colour from green through yellow to red; which are best eaten fresh or which can be stored for long periods. Flavour also varies a great deal. But it is important to choose varieties which suit your local soil and climate: if your favourite variety happens to be one which is not at home in your particular

Apples come in many different varieties, some of which are only locally available.

Some recommended apple varieties

Quinces may be apple- or pear-shaped. They are highly fragrant and golden-yellow in colour.

garden, you are unlikely to have much success with it.

For this reason it's worth looking out for specifically local varieties. These will often not feature in standard nursery catalogues, but will have been bred specifically by generations of local growers in a very limited area. They can be very useful because they have had

Some of the best-known traditional varieties of fruit trees are kept as rootstocks and for breeding other varieties, but their quality or disease resistance may be poor, making them a bad choice for a garden.

Variety	Pick by (month)	Can be stored until (month)	Details
Blenheim Orange	Oct.	Jan.	biennial bearing, large fruit, cooking and dessert; use dwarfing stock
Bramley's Seedling	Oct.	March	heavy cropper, large fruit, excellent for cooking; needs dwarfing stock
Cox's Orange Pippin	Oct.	Jan.	medium-sized fruit, dessert, superb flavour; good soil essential
Crispin	Oct.	Feb.	heavy cropper, large fruit, dessert, can be cooked; use dwarfing rootstock
Discovery	Aug.	Sept.	small-medium fruit, dessert, firm, best-flavoured early
Egremont Russet	Sept.	Dec.	small-medium fruit, crisp, sweet, bitter pit possible; blossom frost-resistant
Greensleeves	Sept.	Nov.	heavy cropper, medium-sized fruit; self-fertile
Idared	Oct.	April	medium-large fruit, dessert and cooking, moderate flavour
James Grieve	Sept.	Oct.	reliable, heavy cropper, large fruit, dessert; good for northern Britain
Jonagold	Oct.	March	fruit can be very large, dessert, crisp, good flavour; vigorous trees
Jupiter	Sept.	March	heavy reliable cropper, medium-large fruit, dessert, Cox's flavour; needs dwarfing rootstock
Katy	Sept.	Oct.	heavy reliable cropper, small-medium fruit, dessert, good flavour; good in northern Britain
Spartan	Oct.	Jan.	crops well, medium-sized fruit, dessert, crisp, good flavour; watch for canker
Winston	Oct.	April	small-medium fruit, dessert, good flavour; good disease-resistance, partially self-fertile

Creating a structure with shrubs

As large fruit trees do not belong in a traditional cottage garden, ornamental shrubs are the next-best thing for imposing a structure on the garden. In the average garden, shrubs are mainly placed around the edges as a kind of hedge. But hedges were traditionally used in cottage gardens only in more exposed areas. In areas where shelter was less of a problem, gardeners made do with individual specimen shrubs.

Old favourites
One shrub which is inseparably associated with country gardens is the **elderberry**. Almost every barn seems to have one growing up against the wall, usually self-sown with the help of birds. If you're not lucky enough to have one growing already, try planting one: it's one of the most versatile of garden shrubs. Its berries attract birds, and in the past its leaves were used to make herb teas and wine, and were baked into pastries. Its berries have a high vitamin content and can be used to make juice, jam or elderberry wine. The wood has a soft pith which can easily be hollowed out to make a whistle, and its roots and bark were also used for medicinal purposes. So it is no

wonder that there was an old farming tradition of raising one's cap as one went past an elderberry bush.

The elder, and other large shrubs, are best planted at the northern end of the garden so that they do not cast shade on other plants. This also applies to the **hazelnut** and the **lilac**. The latter is an excellent example of a foreign shrub whose hardiness and attractive scented blossom have made it a firm favourite in

the traditional cottage garden. The **mock orange blossom** (*Philadelphus coronarius*) is another of these popular introductions from foreign shores. And even if purists say that the brilliant yellow **forsythia** is too garish for a cottage garden, that shouldn't stop you from planting one if you wish.

Some smaller shrubs can look particularly good in a cottage garden provided they do not grow much above fence height.

Hedges: wild or cultivated?

Hedges serve many important purposes apart from shelter, and they may be used in an 'imitation' cottage garden. If you live in a terraced house, you may want the privacy that a hedge can give, and in a large urban garden a wild hedge can provide a home for birds and animals.

However, a wild hedge also takes up more space than a pruned one. If you have enough space, you might grow vigorous

Left *Although introduced from abroad, lilac is almost ubiquitous in cottage gardens in this country.*

Below *Laburnum*

These include the **hydrangea** (*Hydrangea macrophylla* or *H. paniculata*) with its domed heads of flowers. If you are a rose-lover, try shrub roses or delicate wild roses, some of which are repeat-flowering and highly scented, while others have attractive edible rose hips (see page 62).

shrubs around the edges of the garden; in addition to forming a barrier, these also provide protection for birds, insects and hedgehogs, and in many cases their nectar or berries are a source of food. If you have less space but still want a hedge, try growing a small assortment of shrubs along the northern side

Birds often nest in the guelder-rose.

of the garden, perhaps including viburnum, cotoneaster, buckthorn, hawthorn, spindle tree, flowering currant and various wild roses.

A neatly pruned single-species hedge is more time-consuming to maintain, but is denser and provides a uniform background which can set off the bright colours of flowering plants to best advantage. Evergreen box and privet are the most suitable

for this purpose; alternatively, use hornbeam, dogwood or common maple. The dark-green, poisonous yew and the red spruce (*Picea rubens*) are two conifers which may look good in the right place.

But not coniferous hedges
Normally, however, conifers are not suited to cottage gardens. The ubiquitous thuya hedge has no place here. Nor has the savin (*Juniperus sabina*), a close relative of the juniper that has traditionally been popular in some areas. This evergreen creeping shrub has gone out of fashion, partly because of its unpleasant smell and partly because it is poisonous. The Leyland's cypress (× *Cupressocyparis leylandii*) is often planted to form a hedge because it grows so quickly. But it is also time-consuming, and absorbs far too much moisture and plant food.

TREES, SHRUBS AND FRUIT

Ornamental shrubs for the cottage garden

English name	Botanical name	Height in ft (m)	Flowers (month; colour)	Trim to shape	Ever-green	Notes
box	*Buxus sempervirens*	1.5-20 (0.5-6)	*	+	+	very common in cottage gardens
buckthorn	*Rhamnus frangula*	6-13 (2-4)	*	-	-	dark-red berries, tolerates acid soils
cornelian cherry	*Cornus mas*	10-20 (3-6)	Mar.-Apr.; yellow	-	-	easy to grow, red berries, attracts birds and insects
flowering currant	*Ribes sanguineum*	6-10 (2-3)	Apr.-May.; red	-	-	easy to grow, goes well with forsythia, berries attract birds
dogwood	*Cornus alba*	6-13 (2-4)	*	-	-	vigorous, grown for red stems in winter
elder	*Sambucus nigra*	10-20 (3-6)	Jun.-Jul.; white	-	-	very easy to grow and versatile, berries attract birds
forsythia	*Forsythia × intermedia*	6-10 (2-3)	Apr.; yellow	-	-	vigorous, free-flowering
golden rain	*Laburnum* species	16-23 (5-7)	May-Jun.; yellow	-	-	sun or partial shade, poisonous
hawthorn	*Crataegus monogyna*	6-20 (2-6)	May-Jun.; white	-	-	full sun, thorny, attracts birds and insects
hazel	*Corylus avellana*	10-16 (3-5)	Feb.-Mar.; catkins	-	-	nuts in autumn
hornbeam	*Carpinus betulus*	6-20 (2-6)	*	+	+	hedging plant, also tree
hydrangea	*Hydrangea macrophylla, H. paniculata*	6 (2)	Jun.-Aug.; red, white	-	-	attractive flowers, can be pruned
lilac	*Syringa vulgaris*	10-20 (3-6)	May; red, white, purple	-	-	scented flowers, wild form is rampant
field maple	*Acer campestre*	6-20 (2-6)	*	+	-	vigorous tree
mock orange blossom	*Philadelphus coronarius*	10-13 (3-4)	May-Jun.; white	-	-	scented flowers, easy to grow, hedge or specimen shrub
privet	*Ligustrum* species	6-16 (2-5)	Jun.-Jul.; whitish	+	+	easy-to-grow hedging plant, poisonous berries
spindle	*Euonymus europaeus*	10-16 (3-5)	Aug.-Sep.; pink and orange berries	-	-	vigorous, lime-tolerant, has poisonous berries
common spruce	*Picea abies*	6-20 (2-6)	*	+	+	prone to needle drop
viburnum	*Viburnum* species	6-13 (2-4)	May-Jun.; white	-	-	several attractive varieties, some scented; some have poisonous berries
yew	*Taxus baccata*	3-10 (1-3)	*	+	+	various growth habits, conifer, poisonous

* = inconspicuous flowers

Using climbing plants to cover walls

Climbing plants can turn a grey, lifeless wall into a curtain of greenery. If you don't have room for a large tree in your garden, they are also a useful alternative way of creating a vertical dimension. Properly used, they can provide a harmonious transition from the inside of the house to the outside, which is one of the most important requirements of a cottage garden.

Your choice of climbers will be affected by the situation of your own particular garden — what direction it faces, what type of soil it has, what the local climate is like — and also by the area of wall that you want covered. It will also depend on your personal tastes: do you simply want a modest veil of foliage, or do you want to make the plant into a feature in its own right, with large, colourful or scented flowers? The only case that will restrict your choice is a north-facing wall, which will reduce the number of flowering climbers that might be suitable.

Climbing plants create a transition from the house to the garden — in this case highly successful.

There are also fruit trees which you can grow successfully against a warm wall in espalier form: examples include pears, apples and even (if you don't mind taking risks) apricots and peaches. Another plant you can grow against a south-facing wall in milder areas of the country is the grapevine, which rewards careful pruning with its attractive foliage and fruit.

There are also some annual climbers that provide short-term cover for a wall. These include sweet peas, black-eyed Susan and morning glory, all of which can be useful for covering a south-facing wall until you decide what to use in the longer term.

Wisteria — one of the most dramatic of all climbing plants.

Provide a support

Most climbers need some kind of support if they are to cover a wall properly. Only ivy, climbing hydrangea and some forms of Virginia creeper are self-cling-ing and do not need support. Very occasionally this can cause problems if the climber creeps into cracks in the pointing, which can make it crumble away, especially if the plant is pulled off. However, there is not normally any need to worry about this possibility: the climber is much more likely to protect the wall against the effects of the weather than cause any damage.

There are two main types of support used for climbing plants. One is a wooden trellis, which should be fixed about 2–4 in (5–10 cm) away from the wall using spacers. Alternatively, you could use tensioned plastic-coated wire.

Climbing plants

English name	Botanical name	Height in ft (m)	Position	Remarks
clematis	*Clematis* hybrids	6–10 (2–3)	full sun	roots must be shaded
Dutchman's pipe	*Aristolochia macrophylla*	20–32 (6–10)	full sun or partial shade	large leaves
honeysuckle	*Lonicera*	6–20 (2–6)	shade or half-shade	several varieties, some with highly scented flowers
climbing hydrangea	*Hydrangea petiolaris*	16–32 (5–10)	anywhere	self-clinging, large white flower heads
ivy	*Hedera helix*	16–65 (5–20)	does best in shade	self-clinging, evergreen, slow-growing
climbing rose	*Rosa*	6–16 (2–5)	full sun	many varieties, support required
ornamental vine	*Vitis vinifera*	16–40 (5–12)	full sun	some varieties bear edible grapes
Virginia creeper	*Parthenocissus quinquefolia*	20–50 (6–15)	sun or shade	eventually self-clinging, attractive autumn foliage, vigorous
wisteria	*Wisteria sinensis*	20–40 (6–12)	full sun	clusters of blue flowers in May

Cottage-style container plants

The tradition of covering window-sills and balconies with colourful flowers may not be a particularly old one, but it is certainly very widespread. Some villages and suburban streets seem to be engaged in a life-or-death battle for the title of best-decorated front garden.

This type of decoration often tends to be dominated by geraniums, which are sometimes criticised as unimaginative but can look spectacular from a distance. In a smaller container that is closer to passers-by, a combination of plants looks more effective. Large areas, viewed from a distance, lend themselves better to planting with a single species.

The correct botanical name for the geranium is *Pelargonium*, but for the amateur gardener this is largely academic. What is important when planning a cottage garden is knowing the difference between upright forms, grown in either pots or window boxes (*P. zonale*), and forms suitable for hanging baskets (*P. peltatum*).

As geraniums flower so very profusely, they need generous feeding, especially within the restricted space of a container. Many country gardeners are fortunate enough to have access

to large quantities of well-rotted manure, but if you do not, you will need to use liquid feeds.

Ideally, you should propagate about a third of your plants each year by taking cuttings, so that they continue producing plenty of flowers. Snip off the shoot tips in summer and insert them in a free-draining potting compost to root.

But geraniums are not the be-all and end-all: there are plenty of other plants which go particularly well in containers. Some of the most common ones are tuberous begonias, fuchsias, petunias, calceolaria, heliotrope

A luxuriant display of hanging and container-grown plants.

and various species of chrysanthemum. Busy Lizzie (*Impatiens*) is another good container plant, and tolerates shade. But don't be afraid to do your own thing when choosing container plants. What about using the traditionally grown herbs such as rosemary, bay and lavender?

perennial container plants, they should be kept in a well-lit room at 41-50°F (5-10°C).

Many of these plants rely for their effect on being planted in containers, particularly in a true cottage garden. Modestly decorated handmade terracotta pots show them off to best advantage; or use glazed pots for an added touch of distinction. Large, old plants will often be too big for these pots, in which case you might try a wooden tub or barrel, the latter perhaps cut in half. However, if buying purpose-made plant containers isn't your idea of money well spent, try using old catering tins of things like jam or cooking oil. These improvised containers are often used by thrifty cottage dwellers and have a charm of their own, as you will know if you have ever seen them being used in southern Europe.

Flowering plants in pots, bowls and tubs

There are also plenty of exotic plants which can look stunning in containers: oleander, angel's trumpets, New Zealand flax, agaves, yuccas. Of course, none of these beautiful exotics is really a traditional cottage-garden plant, but no one is likely to notice this, let alone point it out.

Some of these exotics will survive the winter out of doors, but to be on the safe side you should overwinter them all in a frost-free position. Like geraniums, fuchsias and many other

A standard form of marguerite

51

Flowering plants — attractive and useful

It is only relatively recently that gardens have become more of a luxury. As people have become more affluent, gardens have become an extension of the living room rather than the kitchen, and we can now afford to grow flowers just for their looks. This would have been regarded as wasteful by our ancestors, for whom the garden was a place for growing edible or medicinal plants. This tradition was preserved for centuries in the cottage garden: there was plenty of beauty in the surrounding landscape, without bringing it into the garden.

Plenty of flowering plants were traditionally grown in the cottage garden, but all of them had some kind of practical use. Of course it could be said that simply looking at plants is a remedy for the stressful existence we lead today. In the past, however, the flowers grown between the rows of herbs and vegetables were mostly medicinal ones.

Marigolds, for example, have long been grown as useful companion plants. But from time immemorial their attractive orange flowers have been used to make a soothing skin ointment and disinfectant. The madonna lily provided a pain-killing oil, while the rhizome of the common German flag (*Iris germanica*) was believed to have a beneficial effect on the digestive system. The flowers of the mullein were used to make a cough mixture, and pansies were made into an infusion reputed to purify the blood. The roots of inula and althaea were once used to make a medicine for throat and lung ailments. Alchemilla and feverfew contain substances which were used to relieve period pain, while the roots of the peony can be used

In addition to its great beauty, the madonna lily is also reputed to have healing powers.

to prevent cramp, and the foxglove contains substances that are used for heart problems.

Of course, self-medication is not always advisable and can even be dangerous. But simply knowing about the healing powers of many flowering plants gives the garden an extra dimension. And many people swear by herbal remedies for minor ailments, which is an understandable trend in view of the rising cost of conventional medicine.

Even weeds have their uses
When country-dwellers in the past allowed weeds to grow, it was not always because they could not keep up with the weeding. Quite apart from the fact that many weeds are modestly attractive, they knew that even these uninvited guests in the garden had their uses.

The stinging nettle could be made into liquid fertiliser (see page 15) for the other inhabitants of the garden. The coltsfoot which often grows on compacted soil, and the plantain which flowers in the fields, were two of the main ingredients of an infusion used to treat coughs and lung problems. Tannins extracted from the narrow-leaved willow herb were used for liver and gall-bladder pains. Stressed country-dwellers made themselves a calming infusion from Saint John's wort. And if you regularly rub the sap from the stem of the greater celandine on warts, they are gradually supposed to disappear.

Above *Peonies were originally grown as medicinal plants.*

Left *Coltsfoot was once used as a cough remedy.*

These are only a few randomly selected examples. But whether or not you are a believer in herbal remedies, so-called weeds often have environmental benefits as well. Many, such as nettles and willow herb, provide an important source of food for threatened species of butterflies and other insects.

Lasting colour in the cottage garden

Cottage gardens often look as though all the plants have seeded at random, but in a good cottage garden a great deal of careful planning has gone into achieving this apparently haphazard effect.

First of all, the plants need to be suited to the location. If the soil tends to be wet, you will not want to grow drought-loving species. In shaded areas, the selection of flowering plants is more limited, but you can achieve some very eye-catching effects with primulas, ground-cover plants such as lily of the valley and woodruff (*Asperula odorata*), ferns and taller perennials such as aquilegia and monkshood.

Most of us have at least a basic idea of which colours go well together. Generally speaking, though, you should use the more muted hues in a cottage garden. By all means have a colourful garden, but not one that dazzles passers-by with its jarring reds, oranges and pinks.

Another important point to bear in mind is height. The place for ground-cover plants and low-growing perennials is at the front of the bed, or between medium-sized perennials in the middle of the bed. Put tall plants at the back to create a background for the rest of the garden and to enable other

people to enjoy the fruits of your labours without invading your privacy by peeking over the fence.

The following are a very small selection of the plants most suited to a cottage garden:

Perennials

Auricula

(*Primula species*)
The lime-tolerant Alpine auricula (*P. auricula*) has yellow flowers, while the garden form (*P. × pubescens*) also has blue and violet strains. Both variants prefer partial shade.

Bergamot, bee balm

(*Monarda didyma*)
The whorls of red tubular flowers are popular with bees. The plant reaches a height of around 4 ft (1.2 m), and has mint-like aromatic leaves that can also be used in cooking.

Bleeding heart

(*Dicentra spectabilis*)
This spring-flowering plant prefers a shaded position. Unfortunately it dies back after flowering and therefore needs to be placed behind larger plants. Its uniquely graceful arching stems make it well worth the effort.

Chrysanthemum

(*Dendranthemum* × *grandiflorum*)
The outdoor varieties of this popular cut flower, with their different colours and shapes of flowers, last from autumn into early winter. They will do best if given plenty of fertiliser and well-drained soil, and will last longer if protected during the first frosts.

Columbine

(*Aquilegia vulgaris*)
With its spurred, multicoloured bell-shaped flowers, the columbine has long been a popular cottage-garden plant. It self-seeds freely, tolerates half-shade and so helps to create a natural-looking effect in the garden.

Left *Lupins in a meadow garden of perennials*

Below *Oriental poppy (*Papaver orientale*)*

Coneflower

(*Rudbeckia* species)
This vigorous genus has yellow star-shaped flowers. Some species (e.g. *R. laciniata*) are medium-height, while others such as *R. nitida* grow to a height of over 6 ft (about 2 m) and belong at the back of the bed. All bloom in late summer. (See picture on page 58.)

Delphinium

(*Delphinium* hybrids)
These elegant columns of often bright-blue flowers add a touch of elegance as well as height to the garden. They are repeat-flowering if you cut them right back after they have flowered in early summer and feed them well. Given a rich soil and plenty of sun, they will grow to a height of 6 ft (2 m) or more.

Elecampane
(*Inula helenium*)
This tall plant was introduced from Asia, and is now natural-ised in some parts of the coun-try. It grows to a height of over 6 ft (up to 2 m), with yellow, daisy-like flowers, and is best grown in a corner of the garden. It is shade-tolerant, and its roots used to be made into a cough mixture.

Evening primrose
(*Oenothera biennis*)
This upright plant was intro-duced from America, and grows to a height of around 2 ft 6 in (80 cm). The bright yellow, cup-shaped flowers appear on warm

evenings from June onwards, and the plant needs a sunny position. It will self-seed freely.

Common male fern
(*Dryopteris filix-mas*)
This native fern, growing to a height of around 3 ft (1 m), was once used as a cure for worms. Like most of its relatives, it is particularly attractive for its delicate leaf shape and the fact that it thrives in shade.

Feverfew
(*Tanacetum parthenium*)
The English name for this plant derives from the word 'febri-fuge', which was a traditional form of medicine used to cure fevers. This highly aromatic perennial naturalises well in a cool place, and looks particu-larly good between roses and medium-height perennials.

There is also a distinctive yellow-leaved form.

Globe thistle
(*Echinops bannaticus*)
This ornamental thistle grows to around 3 ft (1 m) in height, and has vivid blue flower heads which last all summer. It prefers plenty of humus and a fairly sunny, dry location.

Houseleek
(*Sempervivum tectorum*)
The Latin name means 'roof houseleek': this is because the plant was once grown on roofs in the belief that it protected the house against lightning. The leaves were also crushed and used on insect stings and wounds. This plant grows well in poor stony soil. It has fleshy rosettes of leaves and rose-pink flowers.

Tall yarrow provides a blaze of colour for passers-by.

Iris, German flag
(*Iris germanica*)
Also sometimes known as the sword flag on account of its distinctively shaped leaves, this plant has bearded flowers in various shades of blue and violet. Its fleshy rhizomes (once believed to have medicinal powers) must be left uncovered on the surface of the soil so that they get as much sun as possible. The iris also needs well-drained, rich soil. Other irises often used in cottage gardens include *I. sibirica*, which needs damp or boggy soil, and the dwarf bearded iris (*I. pumila*).

Leopard's bane
(*Doronicum orientale*)
This plant produces single yellow daisy-like flowers in spring. It will grow almost anywhere, is shade-tolerant and goes particularly well with forget-me-nots and tulips. The plant reaches a maximum height of about 1 ft 6 in (50 cm).

Lupin
(*Lupinus polyphyllus*)
There are many differently coloured varieties of this plant, which flowers in early summer and should then be cut back to encourage it to spread. It is a nitrogen-fixing plant and prefers poor, acidic soil. Lupins are best propagated from seed. (See picture on page 55.)

Marsh mallow
(*Althaea officinalis*)
This species of mallow eventually grows to a height of about

5 ft (1.5 m), and prefers a cool, damp place in the garden. Its roots were traditionally made into a cough linctus, and its pink or white flowers are popular with bees.

Michaelmas daisy
(*Aster dumosus, A. novi-belgii, A. novae-angliae*)
The Michaelmas daisy was introduced from America, and is now one of the most commonly grown autumn-flowering plants. A. dumosus is a carpeting plant with red, blue or white flowers. The taller species look best at the back of the border, and may need staking. They can be left in the same place for several years if fed regularly. Choose a mildew-resistant variety if possible.

Monkshood, helmet flower
(*Aconitum napellus*)
A highly poisonous native plant, growing to a height of around

Left *Michaelmas daisies are a magnet for butterflies in autumn.*

Right *The old-fashioned charm of phlox*

6 ft (1.8 m). It needs plenty of humus in the soil, and tolerates shade. In summer, it bears hooded dark-blue flowers.

Oriental poppy
(*Papaver orientale*)
Oriental poppies create a dramatic splash of colour in June with their silky bright-red petals and the black blotch in the centre. They are as attractive to insects as they are to humans. Unfortunately, this blaze of glory is all too brief and the poppy soon withers, so it should be placed behind perennials which flower later. (See picture on page 55.)

The late-summer blooms of the coneflower have distinctive cone-shaped centres.

Peony
(*Paeonia officinalis*)
Originally introduced from China as a medicinal plant, the peony is one of the most popular cottage-garden plants. It grows from a fleshy rootstock which dislikes being divided or transplanted. It is a bushy plant with mainly red and white flowers. Do not plant it too deep, and add some well-rotted manure. It was once used to make a remedy for cramp, but it is slightly poisonous.

Phlox
(*Phlox paniculata*)
Many cottage gardeners regard phlox as essential, and this view is borne out by its old-fashioned clusters of brightly coloured flowers in summer. The plant sometimes grows to a height of more than 3 ft (1 m). Unfortunately, some varieties are very susceptible to disease, but you will have the best chance of success if you choose the right variety and plant it in rich, cool soil in a sunny position. (See picture on previous page.)

Pink carnation
(*Dianthus* species)
The Cheddar pink (*D. gratianopolitanus*) bears flowers in various shades of red and pink in early spring above a mat of grey-green leaves. It is followed by the scented *D. plumarius*, which also exists in white. The purple-red flowers of *D. carthusianorum* appear throughout the summer. All of these species grow to a height of 8–12 in (20–30 cm) and prefer well-drained soil.

Ribbon grass, lady grass, gardener's garters
(*Phalaris arundinacea picta*)
The reed-like, white-striped leaves of this ornamental grass are often used in cottage-garden flower arrangements. It prefers a sunny, damp situation.

Shasta daisy
(*Leucanthemum × superbum; Chrysanthemum maximum* of gardens)
This larger relative of the common daisy dominates the garden in summer with its large semi-double white flowers. It needs plenty of sun and well-manured soil.

Sneezeweed
(*Helenium* hybrids)
This undemanding daisy-like plant from North America creates a splash of yellow or red in a sunny herbaceous border. There are several varieties, with different flowering times and heights, though none is taller than about 5 ft (1.5 m).

Yarrow
(*Achillea filipendula*)
This golden-yellow plant grows to a height of up to 4 ft (1.2 m), depending on the variety. It needs a sunny place and rich soil, makes a good cut flower and retains its colour in winter when dried. (See picture on page 56.)

Bulbs

The cottage-garden year begins with snowdrops, crocuses and winter aconite. Gradually, these are replaced by snowflakes and grape hyacinths, and then by tulips and hyacinths with the exotic colours and scents of their native Middle East, and by that quintessential feature of the spring landscape: daffodils. Another even more exotic bulb is the Crown Imperial fritillary, from Asia, with its unusual bell-shaped red, orange or yellow flowers and unpleasant smell, believed to repel voles.

In June the madonna lily (*Lilium candidum*) takes centre stage, with its fragrant white flowers. This is a symbol of purity, and was the first plant mentioned in Charlemagne's *capitulare de villis* (see page 9). It is a particularly important part of the cottage garden, not only for its beauty but also because it flowers well before many other species of lily. The bulbs need a little sand in the planting hole for drainage, and in rural areas they may need a basket placed around them to protect them against voles. Cover the bulbs to a depth of 2 in (5 cm). The

plant reaches a height of around 5 ft (1.5 m), and looks spectacular if planted in groups.

Then, in summer, come the gladioli, which look slightly formal but still have a place in the cottage garden. Finally there are the dahlias, which must be planted out after the last frosts, and whose young shoots will need protection against slugs and snails.

Dahlias provide a blaze of colour well into autumn.

Annuals and biennials

Unlike perennials, whose leaves and stems die back in winter and which live for a number of years, annuals last only one season and then grow anew from seed the following year.

Because these plants are fast-growing, they have the advantage that you can change and modify the layout of your garden each year.

Some of these plants can be sown straight into the soil and will self-seed in a suitable position. Others, especially those introduced from warmer climes, need to be raised indoors in pots in a greenhouse or on a window-sill. They are then planted out in the desired location after the risk of frost has passed, and they will soon come into flower.

While annuals germinate, flower and die in a single season, biennials develop their foliage in the first year and then flower in the second. But it's not always possible to draw such a clear dividing line between annuals and biennials: cosmea and love-in-a-mist often germinate in autumn, and some antirrhinums may regrow from the same plant for several years. Biennials include a number of popular low-growing, spring-flowering plants such as pansies, forget-me-nots and daisies. There are also larger summer-flowering biennials which work best when seen from a distance. These include foxgloves, verbascum and especially hollyhocks. All of them are normally planted out in autumn.

Annuals such as sunflowers allow the garden to be changed round every year.

Annuals and biennials for the cottage garden

English and botanical names	Flowers	Sowing	Other remarks
Annuals			
busy lizzie (*Impatiens walleriana*)	varies	Mar.–Apr., indoors	useful plant for shade, though New Guinea hybrids need sun
China aster (*Callistephus chinensis*)	varies	Mar.–Apr., indoors	prone to disease, needs support, long-lasting cut flowers
cosmos (*Cosmos bipinnatus*)	red, pink, white	Mar.–Apr., outdoors	fine, ferny leaves, single flowers, grows up to 3 ft (1 m) high
French marigold (*Tagetes* species)	yellow, orange	Mar.–Apr.	good edging and companion plant, various heights
love-in-a-mist (*Nigella damascena*)	blue, pink, white	Mar.–Apr., outdoors	self-seeding, seed pods can be used in dried flower arrangements
love-lies-bleeding (*Amaranthus caudatus*)	red	Mar.–Apr., outdoors	unusual long tassels of flowers, typical cottage-garden plant
mallow (*Lavatera trimestris*)	pink, white	Apr., outdoors	attractive trumpet-shaped flowers, very free-flowering
mignonette (*Reseda odorata*)	yellow	Apr., outdoors	attracts bees, highly fragrant
nasturtium (*Tropaeolum majus*)	orange, yellow, red	Apr.–May., indoors or out	climbs to height of 5 ft (150 cm), repels aphids, edible
pot marigold (*Calendula officinalis*)	yellow	Mar.–May, outdoors	important for companion planting, self-seeding
snapdragon (*Antirrhinum majus*)	varies	Mar.–Apr., indoors	sometimes self-seeds, various heights, popular with children
ten-week stocks (*Matthiola incana*)	varies	Apr., indoors	old-fashioned, some double varieties, scented
sweet pea (*Lathyrus odoratus*)	varies	Mar.–May, indoors or out	tendril climber, up to 6 ft (2m), fragrant
Biennials			
daisy (*Bellis perennis*)	red, white (spring–summer)	Jun.–Jul.	good edging plant, perennial normally grown as biennial
forget-me-not (*Myosotis sylvatica*)	mostly blue (spring)	Jun.–Jul.	good edging or filler plant
foxglove (*Digitalis purpurea*)	varies (summer)	May–Jul.	tall-growing, requires partial shade
hollyhock (*Alcea rosea*)	pink, yellow, white (summer)	May–Jul.	striking plant, grows up to 8 ft (2.5 m) high, remove leaves attacked by rust
mullein (*Verbascum* species)	yellow (summer)	Jun.–Jul.	tall-growing, self-seeding
pansy (*Viola* hybrids)	various	Jun.–Jul.	possible to have different varieties flowering all year
sweet William (*Dianthus barbatus*)	varies (summer)	May–Jul.	attracts bees, self-seeding
wallflower (*Erysimum cheiri*)	varies (spring–early summer)	May–Jul.	fragrant, may be perennial if given winter protection

The rose – queen of all the flowers

Roses have been cultivated for thousands of years. They have always been prized for their beauty and the scent of their petals, and have become a symbol of love. They have also had many medicinal and cosmetic uses in the past. Their fruits, rose hips, have a high vitamin content, and can be used to make flavourful jellies, syrups and teas. And children have a less well-publicised use for roses — as a ready source of itching powder.

Today's cottage gardens contain many species which were unknown in the Middle Ages. They are different in many ways from modern bedding rose varieties, which have been bred for brightly coloured, long-lasting petals, and have often lost their fragrance and natural vigour. As a result, some gardeners today feel obliged to use a veritable arsenal of chemicals to protect their roses from diseases like rust, mildew and black spot, and from annoying pests such as aphids and leaf-rolling sawflies.

Old-fashioned roses are more elegant and less susceptible to pests and diseases. The 'English roses' bred by David Austin are vigorous, simple and yet very beautiful, even though most of them are relatively recent creations.

Different growth habits for different purposes

Bedding roses can be planted in a herbaceous border provided the soil is well drained. They combine particularly successfully with lavender, and the etheric oils produced by the lavender can repel some pests. Climbing roses can be grown round your front door or over the garden gate to provide a stylish welcome to visitors. Simple shrub roses look best at the back of the border — or you could make a feature of one by growing it as a specimen, perhaps in a central bed. They can also be underplanted and decorated with a glass ball (see page 25). Standard roses are best suited to this, and can also be placed in rows along main paths. Standards are grafted onto 3-ft (1-m) rootstocks of wild roses or their close relatives.

Looking after roses

The best time to plant bare-rooted roses is October or November, though if you live in a particularly cold area it is probably better to leave planting until spring. Choose a sunny position with plenty of air and well-drained soil.

Before planting, place the roots in a container of water for 12 to 24 hours. Prune any damaged roots or other parts of the plant. Place some well-rotted garden compost in the hole before planting, then fill the

Above *Lavender and roses make a beautiful combination.*

Left *Bush roses covered in flowers can be a breathtaking sight.*

hole with soil and tramp it down so that the bud union is an inch or so below the surface. In the case of standard roses, you should position the supporting stake first.

Any newly planted rose should be protected during its first winter; climbers and standards are especially sensitive to a really hard frost. If the first winter after planting is severe, you could protect them with straw, bracken or plastic bubble sheeting.

Prune the dead stems in March. This is a very easy job with old-fashioned species and varieties. Bedding and standard roses, however, need to have all their shoots pruned, leaving more buds on the stronger shoots than on the weak ones.

The other main requirements of roses during the year are occasional feeding, preferably with well-rotted manure, and watering: don't water the leaves, as this increases the likelihood of disease.

The old-fashioned charm of roses

Every gardener has his or her own particular favourite rose. But the old-fashioned species and varieties have a great deal going for them — not just the fact that they are so vigorous, but also their delicate fragrance and overall appearance, with flowers in soft pastel tones, and dainty, romantic forms and growth habits. All of these characteristics make the old-fashioned roses much better for cottage gardens than luridly coloured hybrid tea cultivars.

'English roses' bred by growers like David Austin combine these features with another desirable trait that has been bred into them: a long flowering period. Repeat-flowering or 'remontant' roses are an intermediate form, producing more than one flush of blooms each summer but still exuding old-fashioned charm.

'Rosa mundi' (top inset), 'Louise Odier' (bottom inset) and a climbing rose.

'Gruss an Teplitz'

Old-fashioned roses

English name	Botanical name	Height in ft (m)	Flowering period	Flowers	Remarks
alba rose	*R. alba*	up to 6.5 (2)	Jun.–Jul.	white–pale pink; double	vigorous, oldest cultivated rose, grey-green leaves, fragrant
Bourbon rose	*R. chinensis* hybrids	5–6.5 (1.5–2)	Jun.–Sep.	red, pink; double	semi-shade, almost thornless, often repeat-flowering
Burgundy rose	*R.* 'Burgundiaca'	2.5–3 (0.8–0.9)	Jun.–Jul.	wine–purple; double	miniature, fragrant, pompom flowers
burnet rose, Scotch rose	*R. pimpinellifolia*	up to 5 (1.5)	May–Jun	white–red; single	ferny leaves, easy to grow
cabbage rose, Provence rose	*R.* × *centifolia*	5–6.5 (1.5–2)	Jun.–Jul	colour varies; double	fragrant, free-flowering, hardy, arching
China rose	*R. chinensis*	4–8 (1.2–2.5)	to Nov.	yellow, red; form varies	front-sensitive, repeat-flowering
damask rose	*R. damascena*	up to 6.5 (2)	varies	colour varies; double	several varieties highly fragrant, some repeat-flowering
dog rose, common briar	*R. canina*	up to 8 (2.5)	Jun.	white–pink; single	many hips, vigorous, thorny
eglantine, sweet briar	*R. rubiginosa*	6.5–10 (2–3)	Jun.	pink; single	arching, apple-scented
gallica rose	*R. gallica*	up to 3 (1)	Jun.–Jul	red; form varies	vigorous, often shade-tolerant, fast-growing, fragrant
moss rose	*R.* × *centifolia muscosa*	up to 6.5 (2)	Jun.–Jul	colour varies; double	mossy stems and buds, fragrant
rugosa rose, Japanese rose	*R. rugosa*	5–6.5 (1.5–2)	Jun.–Oct.	purple–pink; single	full sun, tomato-shaped, large hips

Healthy food from fertile soil

There is an old farming tradition that you should never eat anything you haven't seen growing. Some people might see this attitude simply as an unwillingness to move with the times, but it is one which is becoming increasingly widespread, even among city-dwellers. More and more people are in a position to tailor their menus to what they have available in the garden at any particular time.

When Charlemagne issued his famous *capitulare de villis*, his aim was to increase the variety of plants grown in people's gardens. He did this, not because he was a plant-lover or wanted to achieve greater refinement in what people ate, but rather because he realised that a varied diet would improve their health. His views have been borne out by what we know today: many of the diseases which have afflicted humanity in the past have been the result of a limited diet.

Diversity is no longer a problem in the cottage garden. After a hesitant start, tomatoes and potatoes introduced from America have become an essential part of the garden — and native crops such as cabbage,

beans, onions and the various root vegetables rub shoulders with many plants of Mediterranean origin such as celery, fennel, radicchio and courgettes.

Despite the new willingness to try exotic novelties, we should

still have an eye to our forefathers' eating habits. Some of the vegetables they ate are flavourful and healthy but have been largely forgotten today. Some of these are particularly easy to grow, which is particularly useful given the difficulty of gardening without chemicals. And apart from their nutritional value, they have a firm place in the design of the cottage garden (see page 76).

The ideal cottage garden will provide high yields of a large variety of crops in a small space.

Don't bother digging light or medium soil: just loosen it with a fork.

layer of it onto the soil in spring. The soil can also be improved by adding lime.

On the other hand, heavy, sticky soil prevents water and air from permeating through it, and tends to stay wet for longer periods. If you dig it over before the winter, the frost will break up the clods of earth. Here again, the soil will also be improved by manuring and adding lime.

If your soil is average or only moderately heavy, treat it in much the same way as light soil. Autumn digging will merely disturb it unnecessarily. Add lime only if necessary: large quantities of lime may make a difference in the short term, but in the longer term it can leach the nutrients out of the soil.

To dig or not to dig

Some gardeners dig over their gardens on a piecemeal basis, uncertain whether they should be doing so or not. The question is not one of organic versus conventional gardening: whether or not you should dig depends more on the type of soil.

Don't turn over light, sandy soil, as this will only disturb the ecological balance. All you need to do is loosen it with a fork or hoe, and protect it with a mulch over the winter. If you have access to animal manure, spread a thin

Companion planting – an old cottage-garden tradition

Cottage-garden beds have always contained a colourful mixture of plants, with something crammed into every available space. Carefully combining different species of plants enables you to make the best possible use of the limited space available, both above and below the surface. It also means that as much of the soil as possible is covered, so that it holds more water and makes it more difficult for weeds to grow. The metabolism and food requirements of the different plants play an important part in companion planting — as this method is called — and it also helps to make plants less susceptible to disease.

At the same time, it's important to know which plants can be grown close together in this way and which cannot. For example, if you grow celery and cauliflower together they will improve each other's growth, whereas lettuce grows less well with celery next to it. One of the main principles to follow is that plants belonging to the same family should be kept somewhat apart.

These rules don't just apply to vegetables. The substances contained in many herbs can improve the health of the garden, just as they are believed to cure some human ailments. And some flowers — notably the marigold — are not only a delight to the eye, but can also benefit the plants growing around them.

With careful planning you can always have plenty of vegetables available to provide you with a varied diet.

Marigolds are among the most commonly used companion plants — and not just because of their attractive flowers.

In a true cottage garden, the practice of companion planting is the result of decades of practical experience. If you are relatively new to the business of gardening, use one of the tables

Crops that protect each other

Plant **carrots** with **onions** or **leeks** to repel harmful insects that affect both plants.

Plant **strawberries** with **garlic** or **onions** in order to prevent fungal diseases in strawberries.

Plant **cabbages** with **celery** or **tomatoes**, and the celery or tomato smell will repel the whitefly that lay their eggs on the cabbage.

Plant **carrots** with **marigolds** to repel the nematode worms that cause carrot deformities.

Plant **roses** with **lavender** to repel rose aphids.

Plant **currants** with **wormwood** to prevent currant rust.

Plant **nasturtiums** around **fruit trees** to prevent aphid infestation.

available in many gardening books and magazines — and don't hesitate to ask other gardeners for advice.

Crop rotation

As well as planning your garden to include the right combinations of plants, it is also important to practise crop rotation. You should plan your garden to take account of different growth rates, combining main crops with catch crops. Catch crops are normally those which are fast-growing (e.g. radishes, lettuces, kohlrabi) or winter-hardy (lettuce, spinach etc).

Main crops, on the other hand, take a large part of the summer season to mature.

The main thing to remember is that plants of the same species or family should never be grown in the same place for several years at a time. The few exceptions to this are tomatoes and runner beans, which don't need to be rotated — and of course perennials such as strawberries and rhubarb.

A selection of common vegetables

There is a very wide choice of vegetables available, so lists below include only their main requirements and characteristics. The amount of manuring required (generous, moderate, little or none) is also specified for crop-rotation purposes. Sowing and planting-out times vary greatly from one variety to another, so always follow the instructions on the seed packet.

Planting distances are given thus (to take an example): 6 × 8 in (15 × 20 cm) = 6 inches (15 cm) between individual plants, and 8 inches (20 cm) between rows of plants.

☐ sow Mar.–Apr. under glass, May–Aug. open soil
☐ transplant Apr.–Aug. 9 × 9 in (23 × 23 cm)
☐ don't pick whole plant: pick off leaves as required

Iceberg lettuce
☐ daisy family
☐ generous/moderate manuring

Right *Iceberg lettuce*
Below *Force chicory roots in large pots during the winter.*

Salad vegetables

Cabbage lettuce
☐ daisy family
☐ generous/moderate manuring
☐ sow Feb.–Mar. under glass, Apr. under plastic mulch, May–Jul. open soil
☐ transplant Mar.–Aug. 8 × 10 in (20 × 25 cm)
☐ fast-growing
☐ water regularly
☐ protect against slugs and snails

Looseleaf lettuce
☐ daisy family
☐ generous/moderate manuring

Chicory
- ☐ daisy family
- ☐ moderate manuring
- ☐ sow May–Jun. in rows 12 in (30 cm) apart
- ☐ lift forcing varieties Oct.–Nov.
- ☐ force in pots in darkness (takes about four weeks)

Radicchio
- ☐ daisy family
- ☐ moderate manuring
- ☐ sow Jun.–Aug.
- ☐ transplant Jul.–Sep. 8 × 10 in (20 × 25 cm)
- ☐ pick in autumn or spring

Sugar-loaf chicory
- ☐ daisy family
- ☐ moderate manuring
- ☐ sow Jun.–Aug.
- ☐ transplant Jul.–Aug. 10 × 12 in (25 × 30 cm)
- ☐ fast-growing

Lamb's lettuce/corn salad
- ☐ valerian family
- ☐ moderate manuring
- ☐ sow Jul.–Sep. in blocks or in rows 4 in (10 cm) apart
- ☐ pick in autumn or spring
- ☐ pick individual leaves rather than whole plant

- ☐ sow Mar.–Apr. under glass, May–Jul. open soil
- ☐ transplant May–Aug. 12 × 12 in (30 × 30 cm)
- ☐ fast-growing but crisper and less prone to bolting than cabbage lettuce

Endive
- ☐ daisy family
- ☐ moderate manuring
- ☐ sow Apr.–Jul.
- ☐ transplant May–Aug. 14 × 16 in (35 × 40 cm)
- ☐ tie each head together and blanch under a flower pot before picking
- ☐ water well in dry weather
- ☐ curly-leaved varieties for summer/autumn picking; broad-leaved for winter

Radicchio (top) and endive (bottom) are both late salad vegetables.

Cauliflower, sprouting broccoli
- ☐ moderate/little manuring
- ☐ sow Mar.-Apr. under glass, Apr.-Jun. outdoors
- ☐ transplant Apr.-Jul. 16 × 20 in (40 × 50 cm)
- ☐ fold outer leaves of cauliflower into centre when curd forms

Left *Spinach is a valuable souce of winter vitamins.*
Below *Brussels spouts are very hardy.*

Other leaf vegetables

Spinach
- ☐ goosefoot family
- ☐ generous manuring
- ☐ sow Feb.-Apr. and Aug.-Sep. 6 × 8 in (15 × 20 cm)
- ☐ slightly acid or neutral soil
- ☐ choose mildew-resistant types if possible
- ☐ use for companion planting

Cress
- ☐ mustard family
- ☐ generous manuring
- ☐ sow successively Mar. onwards 3 × 4 in (8 × 10 cm)
- ☐ very fast-growing, takes up very little space
- ☐ can also be grown in a saucer or planter

Rhubarb
- ☐ knotweed family
- ☐ generous manuring
- ☐ plant 'sets' (rootstocks) in Sep.-Oct. 10 sq ft (1 m²) per set
- ☐ perennial
- ☐ can be forced by covering up in late winter

Brassicas

A group of closely related plants belonging to the mustard family. Alternate with salad vegetables, celery, tomatoes, legumes. Prone to club root, cabbage root fly, cabbage whitefly. Seedlings sometimes affected by wire stem (withered, brown stems).

Kohlrabi
- ☐ moderate manuring
- ☐ sow Mar.-Apr. under glass, Apr.-Jul. outdoors
- ☐ transplant Mar.(under glass)-Aug.
- ☐ fast-growing

- broccoli will re-crop if shoots are picked in small quantities
- various colours available

Summer cabbage
- little manuring
- sow Feb.-Mar. under glass, Apr. outdoors
- transplant Apr.-May 20 × 20 in (50 × 50 cm)
- can be cut all year round

Savoy cabbage
- little manuring
- sow Mar.-Apr. under glass, May-Jun. outdoors
- transplant Apr.-Jul. 20 × 20 in (50 × 50 cm)

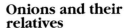

Plaited strings of onions — a traditional storage method

Kale
- moderate manuring
- sow Mar. under glass, Apr.-Jun. outdoors
- transplant Jun.-Aug. 16 × 20 in (40 × 50 cm)
- can be stored after picking, light frost improves flavour

Brussels sprouts
- little manuring
- sow Apr.
- transplant May-Jun. 24 × 24 in (60 × 60 cm)
- needs very firm soil

Chinese cabbage
- moderate manuring
- sow Jul.-Aug.
- transplant Aug. 12 × 16 in (30 × 40 cm)
- eat as a salad vegetable or cooked

Onions and their relatives

Don't use fresh manure. Grow as companion plants to carrots, strawberries and various salad vegetables.

Onions, shallots
- moderate manuring
- sow seed/plant sets Mar.-May or Aug.-Sep. (depending on variety)
- 4 × 8 in (10 × 20 cm)
- shallot leaves edible; onion leaves should be allowed to die back

Leeks
- little or no manuring
- sow Feb.-May
- transplant Apr.-Jul. 6 × 16 in (15 × 40 cm)
- earth up to blanch the stems
- late-season varieties will stand over winter into spring

Garlic
- moderate manuring
- plant Apr./May-Oct. 3-4 × 8 in (8-10 × 20 cm)
- prefers a warm position
- lift when leaves die back

Chives
- Require moderate manuring
- sow Mar.-Apr.
- transplant Apr.-May 8 × 8 in (20 × 20 cm)
- can be kept green over winter by digging up rootstock, allowing it to freeze, then potting up and placing on a warm window-sill

Root vegetables

Potatoes
- [ ] nightshade family
- [ ] little manuring
- [ ] set tubers (seed) to sprout (chit) Feb. in light, cool place 7-9 oz/sq yd (250-300 g/m²)
- [ ] plant Mar.-Apr. 12 × 20 in (30 × 50 cm)
- [ ] hoe regularly after shoots appear, and earth up for higher yields

Beetroot
- [ ] goosefoot family
- [ ] moderate manuring
- [ ] sow Apr.-Jun. in rows 10-12 in (25-30 cm) apart

Radishes
- [ ] mustard family
- [ ] moderate manuring
- [ ] dislikes fresh manure and lime
- [ ] sow summer varieties Jan.-Feb., or Mar.-May outdoors, in rows 15 cm apart, thinning to i in (3 cm); further sowings Aug.-Sep.
- [ ] sow winter varieties Jul.-Aug. in rows 25 cm apart, thinning to 6 in (15 cm)
- [ ] summer varieties very fast-growing and can be used as a marker for slower-growing crops

Fennel
- [ ] carrot family
- [ ] moderate manuring
- [ ] sow Apr.(under glass)-Jul., using a bolt-resistant variety if sown early
- [ ] transplant Jun.-Aug. 12 × 12 in (30 × 30 cm)
- [ ] needs warmth in summer, so place in a sunny, sheltered position

Carrots
- [ ] carrot family
- [ ] moderate manuring
- [ ] sow Mar.-Jun. in rows 10 in (25 cm) apart
- [ ] sow with a quicker-germinating plant such as radishes to mark out the rows, thinning as necessary
- [ ] cover with a net to protect from carrot fly

Celery
- [ ] carrot family
- [ ] little manuring
- [ ] sow Mar.-Apr. under glass
- [ ] transplant May-Jun. 16 × 18 in (40 × 45 cm)
- [ ] keep well watered
- [ ] earth up trench celery; pick self-blanching celery as required

Turnips are tasty and easy to grow.

Parsnips
- carrot family
- little manuring
- sow Mar.-May outdoors, thinning to 6×14 in (15×35 cm)
- feed Jul. with general compound fertiliser
- needs deep, well-drained soil free from stones
- frost improves flavour

Swedes
- mustard family
- little manuring, but add lime if soil is acid
- sow thinly Apr.-Jun. outdoors
- thin early to 9×14 in (23×35 cm)
- water well if conditions are dry
- can be left in ground all winter

Turnips
- mustard family
- little manuring, but add lime if soil is acid
- sow Feb. under glass, Mar.-Jun. outdoors
- thin early to create good-sized roots
- early crop 5×9 in (13×23 cm); main crop 9×12 in (23×30 cm)
- keep well-supplied with water
- start to lift when about 3 in (8 cm) in diameter

Most varieties of pea need sticks as supports.

Legumes

Leguminous vegetables produce their own nitrogen, so they don't require any fertilising at all. Grow them as companion plants to brassicas, lettuces or fennel.

French beans, kidney beans
- sow May-Jul. after last frosts and preferably in dry weather
- 2×16 in (5×40 cm)
- relatively fast-growing

Runner beans
- sow May-Jun. after last frosts and preferably in dry weather

- plant in rows 30 in (80 cm) apart, or 'wigwams' 16-20 in (40-50 cm) apart
- use supports at least 8 ft (250 cm) high

Peas, mangetout
- sow Mar.-May in rows 12-16 in (30-40 cm) apart
- relatively fast-growing; earth up if necessary
- eat the whole pod of mangetout
- twiggy pea sticks needed for support, though there are some self-clinging varieties

Fruiting vegetables

None of these vegetables should be planted outside until after the frosts have passed.

Tomatoes
- nightshade family
- generous manuring
- sow Feb.-Apr. under glass
- transplant May-Jun. 20×32 in (50×80 cm)
- stake plants and keep them regularly watered (water roots, not leaves)
- remove leaves from base of each plant and pinch out side-shoots regularly
- cherry tomatoes particularly flavoursome

Cucumbers
- gourd family
- generous manuring
- sow Apr.-May under glass, Jun. outdoors
- plant out late May-Jun. 16×32 in (40×80 cm)

Rediscovering lesser-known vegetables

Many tasty and nutritious vegetables have almost completely disappeared from gardens, or are present only in their wild form. Their disappearance was brought about by a number of factors such as pest infestation, poor harvests, flavours going out of fashion, or simply the fact that some of these vegetables were associated with hard times and hunger.

But interest in our past has led many vegetable growers to experiment with these traditional crops again. Seeds have become more widely available, and the vegetables described below are very much worth trying, particularly for the traditional-minded gardener.

□ keep well-watered at all times
□ outdoor varieties need a sunny, sheltered spot
□ choose mildew-resistant varieties if possible

Pick courgettes while still young: they taste better and are easier to use.

Courgettes, marrows, pumpkins
□ gourd family
□ generous feeding
□ sow Apr.–May under glass, Jun. outdoors
□ plant out late May–Jun.
□ allow 10 sq ft (1 m²) per plant
□ plenty of warmth needed; often grown on a mound of compost
□ protect against slugs and snails
□ marrows are simply large courgettes

Sweetcorn
□ grass family
□ generous feeding
□ sow Mar.–Apr. under glass, May–Jun. outdoors

□ plant in short rows 12 × 24 in (30 × 60 cm) to aid wind pollination
□ plants need plenty of sun
□ pick when white threads on tops of cobs turn black

Sweet pepper, capsicum
□ nightshade family
□ generous manuring
□ sow Feb.–Mar. under glass, repotting frequently
□ plant out under cloches in May in mild areas 18 × 18 in (45 × 45 cm)
□ plant needs a sunny, sheltered position

Turnip tops, swede rape
(*Brassica rapa, B. napus*)
Turnip tops (also known as turnip rape) and swede rape are the upper parts of the turnip and the swede respectively, and can be used as green vegetables in their own right. Whereas the commoner root vegetables are spaced well apart, the leafy varieties are planted close together to prevent large roots from forming. They can be sown at any time of year, and are ready for picking after about eight weeks.

Left *Cardoon needs to be blanched before picking.*

Right *Ruby chard is highly ornamental.*

Cardoon
(Cynara cardunculus)
This plant grows to over 6 ft (up to 2 m). Like its close relative the globe artichoke, it is thistle-like in form. It is grown for the fleshy ribs of its huge leaves, which are blanched and cooked like asparagus.

Allow around 10 sq ft (1 m²) per plant, and choose a sunny position with rich soil containing plenty of compost. Sow under glass from April onwards, and plant out when all danger of frost has passed. In September, wrap the plants in corrugated cardboard or dustbin liners to blanch them. Pick from autumn onwards.

Swiss chard, spinach beet
(Beta vulgaris flavescens, B. v. cicla)
These vegetables, closely related to beetroot and spinach, have recently become much more popular again after going out of fashion. Part of the reason for this renaissance has been the appearance of attractive new red-stemmed cultivars, although the green-stemmed varieties are also very ornamental. You may prefer the narrow-ribbed leaves of spinach beet, which is used in the same way as spinach, or the fleshy ribs of Swiss chard, which takes longer to cook but has many different uses. Both types are easy to grow provided the soil is well manured. Sow them outdoors from April onwards in rows 12 in (30 cm) apart. The outer leaves can then be picked on a cut-and-come-again basis until winter.

Orache
(*Atriplex hortensis*)
This ancient crop is related to spinach, but is usually regarded as a weed. There are green-, yellow- and red-leaved varieties. All are very easy to grow, and self-seed easily. They also have a very high vitamin-C content.

If you pick individual leaves rather than pulling up the whole plant, a single row will give you a constant supply of salads or vegetables. Pinch out the growing tips (which are often prone to attack by aphids) to encourage the orache to become bushy. Keep the soil damp so that the plant doesn't flower too early.

Sorrel
(*Rumex acetosa*)
Nature-lovers have long known that the leaves of wild sorrel provide a tasty, nutritious and slightly sharp-tasting addition to a salad. But the garden form can also be cultivated: it is an easy-to-grow perennial which will provide a splash of fresh green year after year in the vegetable garden.

Sow the somewhat larger garden form (*R. patientia*) outdoors from March onwards, in rows 12–16 in (30–40 cm) apart. Add compost once a year to increase the yield. Both species can be used either as a salad crop or a vegetable.

Salad rocket
(*Eruca vesicaria sativa*)
This Middle Eastern plant has leaves resembling those of radishes, but their flavour is highly distinctive. Rocket was widely cultivated for centuries, particularly in the Mediterranean region, because it grew so quickly and easily in a well-drained soil.

Sow successively outdoors from April to September in rows 6–8 in (15–20 cm) apart. Pick the leaves before the plant flowers, and use them as a spicy salad ingredient. The plant will self-seed.

Seakale
(*Crambe maritima*)
This perennial plant may not look like a member of the mustard family, but that is what it is. It is native to light, sandy coastal soils, where it was once cultivated as a crop. It needs feeding, but is otherwise undemanding, and can be planted under glass from February or outdoors from April onwards.

There is also a red-leaved cultivar of the garden orache.

It can be propagated by dividing the rootstock. When planted out into its final position, seakale needs about as much space as a large cabbage. Pick the young shoots in spring, having first blanched them under a bucket or similar container. This improves the flavour and enables the vegetable to be cooked or used as a salad. Seakale makes a highly ornamental plant for the vegetable garden when it flowers in May.

Summer purslane
(*Portulaca oleracea*)
A wild form of this native Mediterranean or Indian herb has become established as a weed in this country, where it thrives in light soil and a sunny position. The garden varieties have fleshy shoots and grow to

The leaves of garden sorrel taste excellent and have a high vitamin content.

a height of about 16 in (40 cm). The golden-yellow form is more tender, while the green form has a spicier taste.

Sow summer purslane successionally from May to July, or under glass in April. Plant it in a well-drained soil with plenty of humus, and pick the young shoot tips before the flowers appear. These can either be cooked or used as a salad vegetable.

Jerusalem artichoke
(*Helianthus tuberosus*)
This root vegetable was once grown a lot in cottage gardens. The white or pinkish-coloured tubers of the Jerusalem artichoke have a delicious flavour, slightly sweet, and the presence of insulin makes them a good vegetable for diabetics. The cultivated varieties are less knobbly than the original species.

The plant is easy to grow. Most soils are suitable, and the tubers should be planted in February or March about 6 in (15 cm) deep. The stems grow to over 6 ft (2 m), and in hot summers are topped by yellow, sunflower-like blooms. Dig the tubers from late October onwards, keeping some for replanting. The stems make a good windbreak.

The fleshy leaves of summer purslane can be grown as a salad or vegetable.

Hamburg parsley, turnip-rooted parsley
(*Petroselinum crispum tuberosum*)
Although closely related to the herb parsley, Hamburg parsley is grown primarily for its roots, which have a flavour of parsnip and celery. They are the same colour as parsnips, but about the size of a medium carrot. The parsley-flavoured leaves can in fact be used in the same way as the herb.

Grow in good, well-drained soil in sun or shade, and sow in late March or April, thinning to 9 in (23 cm) apart. Never let the plants run short of water, and start to harvest in November.

Thick-leaved dandelion
(*Taraxacum officinale*)
Dandelions are among the commonest weeds in the garden, and their ground-up roots have been much-used as a coffee substitute. The dandelion's use as a medicinal plant has always made it a familiar plant in the cottage garden. But there is also a cultivated form with thick, fleshy leaves that can be blanched in the same way as endive.

Sow the seed in spring, thinning to 9 in (23 cm) in rows 12 in (30 cm) apart. Then the following spring, cover the new top growth to exclude light. About ten days later, the leaves will be white, making them a first-class vegetable for salads after the winter. Don't continue blanching after June.

Skirret
(*Sium sisarum*)
This perennial is native to southern Europe. It has white flowers and grows to a height of around 32 in (80 cm). The plant has a cluster of roots, each about the thickness of a finger, which have a sweet taste and were widely eaten before the introduction of the potato. Either plant out individual roots, or grow from seed. As the plant is perennial, the roots can be harvested at any time of year. Cut out the woody core, and cook them like salsify.

German rampion
(*Oenothera biennis*)
This biennial plant grows to around 5 ft (1.5 m) in height, and has the typical yellow evening-scented flowers of the evening primrose — the genus to which it belongs. It was introduced from North America and has now naturalised here. In its first year it forms a rosette of leaves above ground, and a fleshy tap root underground, which at one time used to be eaten as a nutritious and tasty vegetable.

Sow outdoors into cool soil in April or May, and then dig up the roots between autumn and the appearance of the first shoots in the following spring. The roots can be eaten raw in salads or cooked as a vegetable. They contain tannins that are used for various medicinal purposes.

Rampion
(*Campanula rapunculus*)
This biennial plant has white, fleshy roots about the thickness of a finger. Sow the seed in June in well-drained soil in rows 8 in (20 cm) apart. The plant is shade-tolerant, but the seeds need plenty of light in order to germinate.

Dig up the roots from October to the following spring, before the violet to blue bell-shaped flowers appear. The roots can be eaten raw or cooked, and the leaves can be used in a similar way to spinach.

Salsify
(*Tragopogon porrifolius*)
This biennial plant is closely related to the yellow goatsbeard (*T. pratensis*), and has the same huge dandelion-like flower. The circle of yellow stylar columns inside the purple flowers gives it a particular charm. The leaves are very similar to those of scorzonera.

This plant is native to the Mediterranean region, but has naturalised in some parts of this country. The fleshy roots and young shoots are edible: they take quite a while to clean, but the flavour makes them well worth the effort. Sow salsify outdoors, and pick either in autumn or spring.

Chinese artichoke, chorogi
(*Stachys affinis*)
This vegetable was formerly cultivated, but fell prey to viral diseases. Since then, however,

more resistant strains have been developed. The plant prefers slightly damp soil, but otherwise needs little looking after. Its roots are small, tuberous and knotty, with a delicate flavour. They should be dug as late as possible in the autumn, and eaten as soon as possible afterwards, as otherwise they will be unusable. Cook them like asparagus or cauliflower, without peeling them.

Scorzonera
(*Scorzonera hispanica*)
This Mediterranean vegetable resembles salsify, both in appearance and use — and its requirements are also similar. Sow outdoors in April in rows 10-12 in (25-30 cm) apart. The plant can be grown all year round. The roots can be left in the soil over the winter, after which the young leaves, or chards, can be eaten.

Little-known food cops — the roots and purple flowers of salsify.

Herbs: a garden full of year-round flavour

Paracelsus, one of the fathers of modern medicine, said that there was a herb for every ailment known in northern latitudes. Many people believe that this is still the case, and although herbal remedies may not be 100 per cent effective,

they can still be used for some simple ailments. What you should not do is resort to them for longer-term self-medication: there is no substitute for seeing a doctor.

Of course, food would not be the same without fresh, home-

grown herbs: dill with pickled gherkins, chives in cottage cheese, basil in pesto sauce, lemon balm in home-made salad dressing, sage used in stuffings, parsley as an edible garnish for potatoes and other dishes, tarragon in vinegar, and Mediterranean dishes flavoured with oregano or garlic. None of these would be complete without the subtle difference created by the addition of fresh herbs.

But we don't just grow herbs for their medicinal or food value. Some are grown purely for their fragrance — especially as aromatherapists and others rediscover the importance of our sense of smell.

Take marigolds, for example. These are often regarded as herbs because they have many uses apart from that of an annual flowering plant. They are good for the soil, and are also believed to be beneficial to the skin, so they are used to make healing ointments and various cosmetics. Other plants such as flax can be used to make clothing. And nature has even provided dyes for these clothes in the form of madder, woad and other plants.

Chives will grow in almost any garden, and its flowers can also be eaten.

Herbs in every corner of the garden

There is no reason why herbs should be confined to a specific part of the garden. In fact a herb garden should consist largely of a small number of perennials such as lemon balm, oregano, tarragon, sage and lovage, with annuals such as marjoram sown between them. Rosemary is not always hardy, and in colder parts of Britain it is best grown in a container and brought indoors in winter. But most other herbs can be grown out in the garden, either in a part reserved for wild plants, or in combination with flowers and vegetables (see also pages 12 and 16).

Savory is best grown between French beans. Dill can be sown between rows of carrots, cucumbers, lettuces or beans, and garlic next to strawberries. Chamomile, caraway, coriander and aniseed should be scattered between rows of vegetables, and rows of cress also make useful companion plants.

Marigolds and borage can be allowed to naturalise in vegetable beds or herbaceous borders. Hyssop makes an excellent edging plant, as do parsley and chives, both of which can also be used as companion plants to lettuce.

Buckwheat (*Fagopyrum esculentum*) can be dug back into the soil as a green manure. Lavender is best if you plant it with roses, perhaps as an eye-catching underplanting in the central round bed of a cottage garden.

Thyme, savory and dwarf houseleeks need a well-drained soil in a rock garden, while peppermint and comfrey need a damp position. Wormwood is said to protect currants against rust. Bryony provides cover for a fence, but this perennial can be invasive.

In a meadow you should allow wild vegetables and herbs to grow, such as dandelions, yarrow, plantain and daisies.

Savory goes very well with French beans, both before and after picking.

Nasturtiums are a particularly versatile herb. They have attractive flowers, which make an ideal edible garnish for salads, and can also be planted underneath fruit trees and bushes to repel aphids and other harmful insects.

VEGETABLES, HERBS AND FRUIT

Cottage-garden herbs

Most herbs grow best in a sunny, sheltered position with light soil. Buy plants, or sow seed under glass in February or March, harden off and plant out in May. Hardy perennials can be sown outdoors in May.

Common and botanical names	Type	How to grow and use
anise (*Pimpinella anisum*)	annual	dried seeds (aniseed) used in baking, confectionery etc.
basil (*Ocimum basilicum*)	annual	pick leaves and use with tomatoes, as a salad ingredient and in pesto sauce; pinch out flowers when they appear
sweet bay (*Laurus nobilis*)	shrub/tree	evergreen, but not fully hardy in severe winters; needs sun and well-drained soil; use leaves fresh or dried
borage (*Borago officinalis*)	annual	young leaves taste of cucumber, and can be used to flavour Pimm's and other drinks; attractive blue flowers can be used as a salad garnish
salad burnet (*Sanguisorba minor*)	perennial	use young leaves in salads and sauces; pinch out flowers; clump-forming
caraway (*Carum carvi*)	biennial	seeds appear in second year, and have various culinary uses
coriander (*Coriandrum sativum*)	annual	pick seeds before fully ripe, and use dried as a spice
cress (*Lepidum sativum*)	annual	sow successionally; can also be grown indoors on a bright window-sill; use fresh leaves as a salad ingredient
dill (*Anethum graveolens*)	annual	well-drained soil; shade-tolerant; use leaves in salads and fish sauces, and seeds in bread
fennel (*Foeniculum vulgare*)	perennial	highly decorative leaves; grows to a height of up to 8 ft (2.5 m); use leaves in soups and sauces
garlic (*Allium sativum*)	biennial/ perennial bulb	divide bulbs and plant cloves in Apr./May or Sep./Oct.; many culinary uses; repels some pests
horseradish (*Armoracia rusticana*)	perennial	plant out shoots or pieces of root; roots used for culinary purposes; plant may be invasive
hyssop (*Hyssopus officinalis*)	perennial shrub	pick leaves before flowering, and use in salads and sauces; clip occasionally to prevent straggling

VEGETABLES, FRUIT AND HERBS

Common and botanical names	Type	How to grow and use
lavender (*Lavandula angustifolia*)	perennial shrub	leaves may be used sparingly with fish, poultry, sauces etc.; flowers used for their scent and to make teas
lemon balm (*Melissa officinalis*)	perennial	pick the lemon-scented leaves before the plant flowers, and use them fresh or dried for salads, sauces and tea
lovage (*Levisticim officinale*)	perennial	pick a few leaves at a time and use fresh in soups and sauces; roots can be used to make tea
sweet marjoram (*Origanum majorana*)	annual	leaves used as a flavouring for meat and vegetable dishes
garden mint (*Mentha spicata*)	perennial	rich, moist soil; sun or shade; keep confined in a large pot sunk in ground; use in mint sauce or with new potatoes
oregano (*Origanum vulgare*)	perennial	pick leaves before plant flowers, and use them as a topping for pasta and pizzas; can also be made into a tea
parsley (*Petroselinum crispum*)	biennial	rich, moist soil; sun or partial shade; species has flat leaves, but most varieties are curly; use as a garnish or in parsley sauce; also makes a good edging plant
peppermint (*Mentha × piperita*)	perennial	rich, moist soil; tends to be invasive; use leaves fresh or dry in mint sauce and mint tea
rosemary (*Rosmarinus officinalis*)	perennial shrub	plant out after last frosts, and protect in severe winters; use leaves in meat dishes and to make tea
sage (*Salvia officinalis*)	perennial shrub	protect in severe winters; use young leaves with fish, roasts etc., or with onion to make stuffing; attractive flowers can also be used as a garnish
annual savory (*Satureia hortensis*)	annual	well-drained soil; pick leaves before plant flowers, and use them with fish and other dishes
French tarragon (*Artemisia dracunculus*)	perennial	rich, free-draining soil; more flavoursome than Russian tarragon; use leaves and shoot tips in salads, vinegar, mixed herbs
thyme (*Thymus vulgaris*)	perennial subshrub	pick leaves before flowering, and use with meat dishes, sauces etc.

Lesser-known herbs

Many useful plants grow un-noticed amid the wild plants in and around the cottage garden. Some are still commonly used as flavourings, herbal teas or for medicinal purposes — ground-elder, garlic mustard, tansy and horsetail, for example. Others have been forgotten or over-taken by the march of progress. Some of these are described below in the hope that they might enjoy a modest revival in popularity after decades of neglect.

Good King Henry has now been replaced by cultivated spinach.

Good King Henry
(Chenopodium bonus-henricus)

This robust perennial is also known as wild spinach or allgood, because nearly all of the plant above ground can be eaten. Even the seeds can be roasted like cereal crops or made into flour. But the leaves are the most important part of the plant: before the intro-duction of its close relative, spinach, this plant fulfilled the same function on account of its high vitamin-C and protein content.

This useful plant often grows unnoticed in the fields, along paths or on rubbish tips. Ideally, it requires rich soil with plenty of humus, and should be sown outdoors in April or May in rows 12–16 in (30–40 cm) apart. The plant produces large numbers of inconspicuous flowers from spring to autumn, and even the flower buds can be used as a delicate salad ingredient. Keep picking the leaves, and eat the young spring shoots as well. Provide a pro-tective mulch in winter.

Agrimony was a valuable medicinal plant in ancient times.

Agrimony, liverwort
(Agrimonia eupatoria)

This was one of the best-known medicinal plants in ancient times. The leaves were used to treat liver pains, gall-bladder ailments and bleeding. The downy stem grows to a height of around 3 ft (1 m), and bears a spike of yellow flowers. It has aromatic leaves and roots, but the ancients used it for its tannic-acid content.

Agrimony prefers light soils. The seed can be very difficult to germinate, so it's best to obtain a young plant.

Buckwheat
(Fagopyrum esculentum)

Although closely related to rhubarb, buckwheat was in fact grown as a cereal thousands of years ago in Asia and elsewhere. In Europe it grows mainly on poor sandy soils or peat bogs. Its seeds have a high starch and protein content, and it was used to make flour for pancakes, bread and other foods. Today it is sometimes used as a green manure as part of a crop-rotation system, where it is more effective than any of its relatives in the knotweed family.

Left *Buckwheat was once grown as a cereal, and is often used as a green manure today.*

Right *Flax provides both oil and fibres.*

Buckwheat is normally sown after the last frosts, on a well-drained, lime-free soil. You can also sow it as a green manure any time until August, though it will invariably be killed by the first frosts.

Flax
(Linum species*)*

From the dawn of agriculture down to relatively recent times, flax was the main plant used to make fabrics. It is enjoying something of a revival at the moment, as linen is back in fashion as a clothing material. The plant is relatively easy to cultivate, and fits in well with a crop-rotation system. The seeds have long been recognised as a healthy source of nutrition, while the oil also has a number of technical uses.

Flax has never entirely disappeared from gardens, because there is a popular ornamental perennial *Linum perenne* that has attractive sky-blue flowers. Flax has also continued to be grown for its seeds, though the oil is obtained mainly in warmer regions. In fact, the plant has so many different uses that a number of different cultivars have been developed.

The annual European flax *Linum usitatissimum* should be grown on cool, well-drained soil. Sow from late March onwards. The unbranched shoots grow to a height of around 3 ft (1 m), and flower in early summer.

Madder is still used to make a red dye.

Soapwort was once used for washing clothes.

Madder
(Rubia tinctoria)

This Mediterranean plant has been used to make a red dye since ancient times. Although bushy, it will also grow upwards if supported, and has yellow flowers that open in midsummer. The red dye is made from a substance contained in the bark of the root; it has largely been replaced by synthetic dyes.

Although madder prefers a warm, dry site in its natural habitat, it is best grown in a cool position in the garden. The best method of propagating it is by rooted runners, and the area between the plants should be regularly weeded. Madder is a perennial, but should be protected in severe winters, assuming it hasn't been dug up in autumn for its roots.

Woad
(Isatis tinctoria)

A member of the mustard family, this plant comes from the Middle East but has naturalised in this country. At least two thousand years ago, long before the introduction of indigo, woad was the source of Europe's most coveted blue dye. The blue colour was obtained by processing the leaves.

The plant requires a well-drained and well-manured alkaline soil, and likes a warm, dry position. The 3-ft (1-m) stem grows above a rosette of leaves in the second year. The yellow flowers appear in spring.

Soapwort, bouncing bet
(Saponaria officinalis)

As the name suggests, the roots of this common European perennial were used to make a kind of soap for washing clothes. It was also believed to cure coughs and other illnesses.

Soapwort grows to a height of just over 20 in (50 cm). It has light-pink or white, double or single flowers which on warm summer evenings exude a delicate scent — a feature that has made it more popular in recent years. The plant is also very attractive to insects. It will grow on any average soil, and spreads by means of fast-growing creeping rhizomes, so is best propagated by division in spring.

Motherwort, once an important medicinal plant, is now a significant source of food for insects.

Motherwort
(Leonurus cardiaca)

Also known as lionheart (hence its Latin name), this plant was introduced from Asia and has partly naturalised. It is an upright plant up to 4 ft (1.2 m) in height, and bears pale-pink to purple labiate flowers in the leaf axils throughout the summer, providing a popular source of food for bees. The leaves contain various substances that have long been used to treat heart and other ailments; it's not yet fully understood how these substances work.

Motherwort is a perennial, and prefers a sunny, well-drained position, preferably underneath other wild plants or up against a fence. It has no other particular requirements. The plant can also be made into a herbal tea that is reputed to have calming properties — although it's not suitable for long-term self-medication. Motherwort is also attractive to insects.

Easy-to-grow soft fruit

Soft fruits don't strictly belong to the ancient cottage-garden tradition. They have only been cultivated on a large scale in the past two hundred years or so, and even then in fields rather than gardens. But they do meet many of the criteria for a good cottage-garden plant: they are easy to grow, will thrive in semi-shade underneath tall trees, and will naturalise on land not suitable for many other crops. They fulfil a dual function as hedging and food plants, requiring little care but providing a rich harvest.

Admittedly, some of them aren't easy to pick — notably the small currants, where a cluster of fruit has to be removed from the bush, then laboriously picked off one by one and washed. Many people in today's fast-paced society have neither the time nor the inclination for this kind of chore, and so soft fruit have become less common in modern gardens. But they are still popular in some circles, and this may have something to do with their nostalgia value. Most people can remember those tempting red or black fruits that they once picked in their grandparents' gardens, often making the painful discovery that these sweet fruits were protected by sharp thorns.

Planting and mulching

Currants and blackberries should ideally be planted in October or November. But if the garden soil is heavy, raspberries and gooseberries are best left until March. They make good cover for the area immediately inside or outside the fence.

Dig the hole deep enough to ensure that there is plenty of room for the roots after pruning, and place some well-rotted garden compost in the bottom to get the plant off to a good start. Water round the base of the plant, and then provide a mulch as soon as possible. This is one of the few jobs you will have to do, and means you will have to do a lot less watering later on. You should mulch currants and gooseberries with grass cuttings or similar material, and the faster-growing blackberries and raspberries with composted bark.

To propagate from existing bushes, remove rooted suckers from raspberries in autumn, and replant them in the place where they are to grow. Take hardwood cuttings from currants and gooseberries in October, and insert them in a sheltered

place outdoors, planting them out the following autumn. Pin down the tips of new blackberry shoots in summer, and plant them when they have rooted properly.

Right *A rich harvest of redcurrants*

Below *Mulching is essential for a good crop.*

Regular pruning

The most important thing you can do to ensure a bumper harvest every year is to prune the bushes. Cut back fruited and dead stems to ground level, leaving only a few fruited canes to encourage new ones to grow and fruit. As blackcurrants mainly fruit on the previous year's new stems, you should cut back the older branches to side shoots. In the case of raspberries, take the opportunity to remove diseased stems in late winter before new growth begins. Also, remove the fruited canes to ground level immediately after fruiting.

Strawberries require very different treatment from other soft fruits. They are usually planted in August or September between vegetables and flowers. If grown intensively they will only fruit well for two to three years, after which they should be replaced by newly propagated plants.

A cornucopia of soft fruit

Redcurrants and whitecurrants

These two fruits (the latter being a mutation of the former) are less commonly grown and sold than blackcurrants. They are equally delicious, however, and one bush will produce large quantities of fruit if well cared for. There are many varieties,

Picking blackberries can be fun, but you must choose a compact variety if you don't want them to take over the whole garden.

each with its own specific fruit size, growth habit, hardiness, sun requirements and flowering time. Redcurrants are more acidic in flavour, making them most suitable for jellies, jams and pies; whitecurrants can be eaten fresh.

Blackcurrants

Blackcurrants produce slightly fewer fruit than their red and white relatives, but they have a higher vitamin-C content and they are often thought to be

tastier. This is why they are sometimes added to redcurrant jelly for extra flavour. Blackcurrants are also ideally suited for making juice and syrups.

Gooseberries

There are two main types of gooseberry: culinary and dessert. Culinary varieties are sharper, and are picked while still unripe for use in pies and jams, while the sweeter dessert varieties can be eaten fresh. Plant more than one variety to

ensure fertilisation. Gooseberries are easier to grow than many other soft fruit, though prone to mildew. Diseased or dead wood needs to be pruned. They also dislike wet soil.

Loganberries

This successful cross between a raspberry and a blackberry produces long, dark-red fruit that is sweet when really ripe and delicious eaten fresh. Loganberries are also very good for making pies and jams, so are well worth trying if you like to experiment in the garden. The fruits appear in July and August. There are many other hybrid berries that are worth growing.

 Standard-grown soft fruit is grafted onto a strong, straight rootstock about 3–4 ft (1–1.2 m) high. This is mainly done with gooseberries. Standard-grown fruit is easier to pick, and the bush is easier to prune. It also looks highly decorative, for example, if you plant several standard gooseberry bushes along both sides of a path. And if you don't want to waste even an inch of space, plant something else underneath the bush.

Raspberries

Raspberries are the most popular of the cane fruit. They are expensive to buy in shops because picking them is time-consuming and they do not transport well, so there is much to be gained by growing them in your own garden. If you don't have a garden that is big enough to let them run wild, plant them in rows and support them from the second year onwards, using wires stretched between posts. There are two types of raspberry: the summer-fruiting varieties, which have a shorter fruiting period but higher yields; and the autumn-fruiting varieties. Raspberries have more uses than any other garden fruit, and can also be frozen.

Blackberries

The wild bramble is a common sight in the countryside and on

Blueberries are rarely grown in this country. They need acid soil.

derelict land in towns, but it is a rampant grower and the thorns can make it difficult to pick the fruit. However, modern growers have produced compact (and in some cases thornless) hybrids that are more suitable for gardens. The fruit has a high vitamin content, and can be put to many different uses.

Blueberries

The highbush or cultivated blueberry has larger fruit than the wild species, commonly known as bilberries. The bush grows to about 3–5 ft (1–1.5 m), and may bear several pounds of fruit after only a few years. But it's not always an easy plant to grow: moist, acid soil is essential, which in most cases will mean adding peat.

Compost — the life-blood of the garden

Compost heaps are all the rage these days. Express an interest in a gardener's compost heap, and he or she will enthusiastically expound its virtues for hours on end, given half a chance. The recent renaissance of the compost heap has a great deal to do with the growing interest in environmentalism. Transporting all organic waste to landfill sites is acknowledged to be both costly and wasteful of resources, and one of the simplest ways of reducing waste output is to return it to the soil from whence it came. Some local authorities have even found that it pays to give away compost bins rather than collect mounds of potato peelings every week.

Once you have a compost heap (and a wheelbarrow for shifting the compost), the only other things you will need to keep your garden healthy are a watering can and a hose. You might have to add substances such as lime to improve any deficiencies in the soil, but compost is a living substance that in sufficient quantities will give your plants all the nutrients they need.

Where to site your compost heap

Choosing a location for a compost heap may not always be easy. Much depends on the space you have available. For aesthetic or practical reasons, you may not want to put it close to your house — and yet you don't want to have to walk a long way every time you put a few weeds or kitchen scraps onto it. If you have a small garden in a built-up area, you may not have much choice as to where you put it.

You will also need to decide whether to use an open compost heap or a bin. The former costs little or nothing, and will do a perfectly good job. In a smaller garden where space is at a premium, you may prefer to use a bin, or possibly two bins, as these take up less space and can look tidier. However, a closed container is not the ideal solution: the rotting process is harder to control here because there may not be enough air and humidity inside. Moreover, modern-looking plastic containers can look very out of place in a cottage garden.

Damp and well ventilated

Wherever you site your compost heap, it should be placed in the shade of a large shrub, such as an elder or hazel, rather than in bright sunshine. This will ensure that the compost doesn't dry out. The two most important requirements for rotting to take place are dampness and nitrogen, so a container should allow plenty of air in. However, the material should never be allowed to get so wet that air is excluded, so the soil base should afford good drainage. The best way of starting the compost heap is to

Above *A simple but effective wooden enclosure for a compost heap*

Left *Plenty of garden compost makes for a full, healthy garden.*

put some large branches and sticks underneath so that air can circulate through it.

Don't put large items into the heap, as these will take longer to rot: use a shredder if necessary. The ideal mixture is a balance between strawy, woody material and green waste that contains sap and nitrogen. If you have access to manure, then put this in as well to improve the compost, but add plenty of straw or wood chippings. As the compost matures, you should cover the heap so that the nutrients aren't leached into the ground by heavy rain.

 Most organic waste materials can be used to make compost, but with a few important provisos. Citrus-fruit peel often contains large amounts of pesticides and preservatives, which in small doses will break down in the compost heap — but don't add large quantities of orange or lemon. Meat, fish and other cooked food waste will attract rats and other animals, so should be avoided.

Index

agrimony 87
annuals 60
apples 43
arbours 35
arches 24
auricula 54

bark mulch 29
beans 75
beetroot 74
benches 19, 34
bergamot 54
biennials 33, 60
blackberries 90, 93
blackcurrants 90, 92
bleeding heart 54
blueberries 93
box 8, 32
brassicas 72
buckwheat 87
bulbs 59

cardoon 77
carrots 74
celandine 13
celery 74
Chinese artichoke 81
chives 73
chrysanthemum 55
clematis 25
climbing plants 48
columbine 55
companion planting 16, 68, 83
compost 15, 94
coneflower 55
conifers 38, 46
container plants 19, 50
corn salad 71
courgettes 76
cress 72
crop rotation 14
cucumbers 75

dahlias 59
damsons 42
dandelion 80
delphinium 55
digging 67
dormice 16
dry-stone walling 21

edging plants 32
elderberries 44
elecampane 56
espaliers 48
evening primrose 56

fences 20-23
fennel 74

fern 56
fertilisers 15, 53
feverfew 56
flax 88
forsythia 45
fruit 37, 90
fruit trees 37
fruiting vegetables 75

garlic 73
geraniums 50
globe thistle 56
Good King Henry 86
gooseberries 90, 92
gravel 28
ground-cover plants 33

hanging baskets 50
hazelnut 44
hedges 44
herbs 82
honeysuckle 25
horse chestnut 38
houseleek 56

iris 57

Jerusalem artichoke 79

lamb's lettuce 71
leaf vegetables 72
leeks 73
legumes 75
leopard's bane 57
lettuce 70
lilac 44
loganberries 93
lupin 57

madder 89
madonna lily 27, 52, 59
manure 14, 95
marigolds 52, 61, 83
marsh mallow 57
medlar 42
Michaelmas daisy 57
mock orange blossom 44
monastery gardens 9
monkshood 57
motherwort 89

nutrients 15, 94

onions 73
orache 78
orchard 40
oriental poppy 57

parsnips 75

paths 26-31
peas 75
peonies 52, 58
perennials 54-58
pesticides 4, 53
pests 16
phlox 58
pink carnation 58
potatoes 74
purslane 79

quinces 42

radishes 74
raspberries 90, 93
redcurrants 92
rhubarb 72
ribbon grass 58
Romans 6
roses 24, 25, 45, 62-65

salsify 80
savin 46
scarecrows 17
scorzonera 81
seakale 78
service tree 42
shade 19, 54
shasta daisy 58
shrubs 44
slugs 17
snails 17
sneezeweed 58
soapwort 89
soft fruit 90
sorrel 78
spinach 72, 86
spinach beet 77
standard rose 25, 63
strawberry 91
swede rape 76
swedes 75
sweetcorn 75
Swiss chard 77

tomatoes 75
trees 36
turnip tops 76
turnips 75

vegetables 66-81

water containers 31
whitecurrants 92
wild flowers 13
wild spinach 86
wire netting 20
woad 89

yarrow 58